Following Evidence to Jesus

Following Evidence to Jesus

And Leaving Behind Doctrine and Theology

JOHN ZAVICAR III

RESOURCE *Publications* • Eugene, Oregon

FOLLOWING EVIDENCE TO JESUS
And Leaving Behind Doctrine and Theology

Resource Publications
An Imprint of Wipf and Stock Publishers
199 W. 8th Ave., Suite 3
Eugene, OR 97401

www.wipfandstock.com

PAPERBACK ISBN: 979-8-3852-7044-6
HARDCOVER ISBN: 979-8-3852-7045-3
EBOOK ISBN: 979-8-3852-7046-0

VERSION NUMBER 02/03/26

Contents

Preface

THE DOCUMENTATION OF JESUS presented in the Bible is the most fascinating account of a person that has ever been written. The Gospel records in the Bible claim that Jesus is God who came to the world in the form of a man to be a sin sacrifice. They record that Jesus was hung from a cross and pierced, resulting in his death, then he was entombed and resurrected himself. If that documentation can be believed, Jesus is the only person ever to have died and come back to life, and we are to pay close attention to Jesus' words. If the documentation cannot be believed, Jesus is just one more urban legend story that is interesting fiction.

Scholars and so-called 'experts' unanimously claim that Bible documentation about Jesus presented in the Gospels came from verbally passed down stories that many refer to as 'oral traditions.' In addition, they estimate the Gospels to have been written twenty to fifty or more years after Jesus was executed. Oral tradition and accounts written many years after the events took place are not indicative of reliable testimony. To make the story of Jesus even less believable, all four Gospels are anonymous. To an assessor, analyst, and fraud inspector like me, the stated Gospel origin theology and lack of evidence cause doubts about the story of Jesus. In addition, the lack of evidence supporting the Christian faith makes it an easy target for ridicule and disbelief by most people.

Due to the apparent lack of evidence supporting Jesus, ancient Christian religious leaders have created theology to present the Gospels to the world as eyewitness testimony. The Gospel of Mark is stated to be Peter's testimony, documented by a man named John Mark, who never witnessed Jesus himself. The Gospel of Matthew is presented as eyewitness testimony from a tax collector named Matthew, who became a disciple of Jesus. His prolific copying from Mark has been explained to be because he, like the rest of the disciples, revered Peter. The Gospel of Luke is attributed to a meticulous doctor who never met Jesus, but he interviewed eyewitnesses and documented their testimony. The Gospel of John is stated to have been written by John, a disciple of Jesus who was with Jesus but waited to document his testimony until many years after the life of Jesus. The theological package of Matthew, Mark, Luke, and John might convince some to believe, but two out of four are stated to be second-hand accounts. In addition, even a quick review of this claimed authorship, which came from the ancient Christian religious leaders also referred to by many as "Early Church Fathers," finds no solid evidence to support it.

Without solid evidence to prove the accounts of Jesus to be true, Christian religious leaders needed fool-proof theology, so they claimed the Bible to be the inerrant and infallible word of God. This theology became a standard for much of the Christian church. However, it is a circular argument that demands Christians believe the Bible to be the word of God without question. They claim that the words in the Bible are the word of God, so the accounts of Jesus MUST be true. But this is the same argument used by Muslims and others who have a book they claim to be the word of God. So, if you believe this Christian theology, you should also believe those promoting other religions, too.

For many years, I tried very hard to accept the Christian theological package, and it worked for a while. But as time went on, my thorough studying of the Bible revealed numerous contradictions, so I doubted the Bible's claim. With it, I doubted the validity of the accounts of Jesus. After a near-death experience in 2020, God prompted me to start an investigation to search for the truth. Regardless of my results, as with any of my numerous investigations, I was out to find and report only the truth.

In summary, my investigation results proved the Bible to contain the inerrant and infallible word of God. However, portions of the Bible do not meet God's requirements to be considered the word of God. Specifically, I found that two of the four Gospels—Matthew and Mark were not authored by those whom early church fathers claimed to be the authors. Their true authors, together with John, the author of the Gospel of John, were disciples of Jesus who wrote their eyewitness testimony immediately after Jesus' resurrection. The evidence package presented in these investigation results proves beyond any reasonable doubt that Jesus is God who came to the world in the form of a man, and that people would be wise to follow his words.

I have found the truth, and I believe in Jesus. If you already believe in Jesus and are reading these investigation results, you will be comforted to find that the Jesus you believe in is proven through solid eyewitness testimony. None of my results damages the story of Jesus—in fact, it supports and confirms it as the truth. However, you have been taught to find Jesus through theology, rather than evidence. It might be difficult for you to let go of the theology you have been accustomed to, but if so, you must simply realize that you don't need it, because you now have evidence.

On the flip side, if you have rejected Jesus in the past for lack of evidence, you owe it to yourself to carefully consider the evidence package to see if it changes your mind. You should realize that with Jesus proven to be God, you can be assured that the judgment, heaven, and hell that Jesus spoke of are also true. When your short time on earth reaches its end, you will either be rewarded through eternity in heaven or you will be condemned and punished to an eternity of everlasting pain and agony in the lake of fire. I suggest you carefully consider the evidence and choose your path forward wisely!

Abbreviations

AOD—Abomination of Desolation

ART—Antichrist, Rapture, Tribulation theology

CRL—Christian Religious Leader

ECF—Early Church Father

JB—John the Baptist

LANL—Los Alamos National Laboratory

LPG—Liquid Petroleum Gas

NC—New Covenant of Jesus

NDE—Near-Death Experience

NT—New Testament

OC—Old Covenant

OT—Old Testament

1

Our Creator Is a God of Evidence

Requiring evidence to prove that God exists and Jesus came to the world as God in human form is not a bad thing. In fact, there are two major reasons for evidence to be expected. First, the Old Testament (OT) focuses on evidence to prove God's presence among his creation of people. God proved to Moses, the Egyptians, and the Jewish people that he existed and was present with them through numerous miracles. As examples, the Egyptians witnessed the plagues, and the Jewish people witnessed the parting of the Red Sea and manna from heaven as food God provided them during their forty years in the desert. Through their personal observations of these miracles, they had the evidence to believe in God. Similarly, the New Testament (NT) documentation provides examples of Jesus performing numerous miracles, such as bringing people back from the dead and resurrecting himself. Those who witnessed Jesus' miracles had the evidence to believe in him. But this OT and NT evidence was only good for those who witnessed the miracles—it is not evidence for future people unless the documentation of these miracles in the Bible can be validated as being true.

Second, people expect solid evidence from a God who created the world. There are many accounts from people who have claimed that God has personally provided evidence of his existence through miracles. I am one of those people who God blessed with personal evidence to prove he exists. I didn't always attribute my seemingly miraculous events to God. In my teen years, I received numerous strange 'prompts' that came from nowhere but had me take specific and quick actions to avoid certain death. But I didn't recognize God in these events because I wasn't looking for him. When events such as someone attempting to run me over with their car and my own personal reckless behavior didn't kill me, I attributed being kept alive to karma.

Then, in my late twenties, God made it impossible for me to continue to ignore him. A year after I started working in an oil refinery in 1985, I completed an engineering modification project at a liquid petroleum gas (LPG) tanker truck loading rack, which required operator training. The training session was to begin at 9:00 am on a Sunday morning, but my alarm clock failed to wake me. I immediately called in to cancel the training and asked the lead operator to reschedule the training for a later date. At about 9:15 am, while still at home about three miles away from the refinery, I heard a loud boom and the ground shook as though a bomb had exploded nearby. About fifteen minutes later, I received a call from my boss telling me that there was an explosion at the LPG loading rack and I needed to get there immediately to help.

The death and destruction at the site were overwhelming. The training site and surrounding area looked like a war zone with devastating damage. Massive amounts of twisted pipes surrounded a blown-out control room. Half of a semitruck-trailer that had been loading LPG had been torn away and was missing. I walked past a vehicle marked, "Coroner", then came up to two men near what was left of the truck; one wearing a coroner's jacket. The two men were standing over the bodies of two workers who had been killed, and they cautioned me about looking down. I followed their advice.

My scheduled training class would have been at the immediate location where the two bodies were found. Later, when I returned home, I shook as I closely examined my alarm clock. I tested it multiple times and found nothing wrong with it—the time was set right, and the clock was functional. It just mysteriously hadn't alarmed that morning. Had my alarm gone off that morning as expected, there is no doubt that at the time of the explosion, I and several operators would have been standing next to that truck and would have been shredded into pieces like the two men who died.

It was on that day that I knew God was in charge and had spared my life. I could no longer ignore God's presence. It wasn't a coincidence that around the same time, God provided me a devout lifetime Christian wife. I felt blessed, and not too long after this event, while dating my soon-to-be wife, I started to search for the word of God.

God had provided me evidence that he was with me, so I expected to find additional solid evidence telling me about God's expectations. I started studying the foundation for various religions and found that the Bible had the best chance of providing me with solid evidence for God. There were numerous miracles presented in it, and there were four Gospels that were claimed to be eyewitness testimonies of Jesus. Several years later, I became a follower of Jesus, but with doubts about the Christian Religious Leader (CRL) theology they presented to claim the story of Jesus to be true.

Then, almost fifteen years later, God provided me another important piece of evidence to prove his existence. In 1999, a few weeks before moving nearly 1500 miles for a new job, my wife's best friend revealed heartbreaking news that the treatment for her terminal cancer had failed. She was now terminal with a short time remaining to live. With sadness, we said goodbye, knowing that we would probably not see her alive again.

About a month later, in our newly purchased home, something very strange happened. After falling asleep one night, I was stirred in bed by something hovering over me that appeared to have a form, yet it also appeared to be formless—if that makes sense. After I realized I was fully awake and was observing an 'entity' floating over me, I started swatting at it while screaming, "Get away." But my shouting and swatting had no effect. My actions woke my wife, who frantically and repetitively asked me, "What's wrong?" I kept yelling back at her, "Something's floating over me and it won't go away." Out of desperation, I jumped out of bed, turned on the light, and the 'Spirit' was gone. We talked for a few minutes about how weird this experience was, then we both went back to sleep.

We woke up the next morning to the phone ringing. My wife answered the phone, and I overheard her mother break the news to her that our friend had died during the night. They discussed the vision I had about the same time she had died, but they didn't seem to be surprised because they were both devout believers in Jesus, just like our friend was. We all knew that our friend was visiting me to say goodbye. During this event, I was shocked, but our friend, who was now in spirit form, appeared to me as though she was on a very peaceful journey to heaven. The message was very clear that there is life after death, and a follower of Jesus, like her, will have an eternal existence in peace.

Through these two events, God had provided me evidence that he existed, was with me, and that there was peace after death for those who followed Jesus. What I was supposed to do with this information puzzled me for many years. Then I found out through one more solid piece of God-provided evidence. The day after COVID shut everything down in March of 2020, my life changed.

I went into a hospital for extensive emergency surgery to repair my severely damaged back. The back surgery went fine, but the anesthesia and recovery process, which was affected by the COVID staffing, caused me to have a major frontal lobe stroke. I later found out that most people die from the stroke I experienced. What I witnessed during that event was completely opposite of how I felt when our friend was on her way to spend eternity with God. It was as though I was in hell for hours upon hours. My world was full of darkness, and although I could see the light of God in the distance, it would not approach me, and I couldn't reach it. A minute in this place of pain and hopelessness seemed like a lifetime, and I knew that if I didn't live, every second of my future for eternity would be like this experience.

I continued praying throughout my near-death experience (NDE), and the seconds morphed into minutes, then the minutes morphed into hours, then the next morning, I finally realized that God had spared my life. I thought about the words of Jesus that hell was like the "weeping and gnashing of teeth," and I knew it to be true.

At the time of my NDE, I was not a novice Christian, as I had over thirty years of in-depth studying of the Bible. I knew that the story of Jesus was outstanding, but the CRL theological package proving Jesus to the world failed miserably. Over the years, God had proved himself to me through solid evidence, but CRLs were trying to prove God to me through theology—something was wrong and that something was sending me to hell if I didn't do something about it.

I had the skills to search for the truth for many years, but I did nothing. Throughout my career, God had molded me into an engineering systems analyst who was skilled at solving operational and maintenance problems that others had tried and failed. Midway through my career, Los Alamos National Laboratory (LANL), arguably the premier research and development facility in the world, hired me as a Subject Matter Expert (SME). With top-secret clearance, I was counted on to review and evaluate all aspects of LANL administrative functions and nuclear/personal safety and security performance.

God ensured that I obtained the perfect job training and experience I needed to go to work for him. LANL managers requested my expertise to "fix the broken" Waste, Fraud and Abuse Investigations Group process. The interrogation training I received from the Federal Bureau of Investigation ensured that I had the skills to evaluate witness statements and determine the truthfulness of witnesses and suspects. These skills were perfect for undertaking an investigation to determine what happened to an expected evidence package for Jesus that, 2000 years later, was a CRL theological concoction of a story about Jesus.

The NT Gospels are supposed to be Jesus' witness statements, and God molded me into a recognized expert analyst and investigator with the skills to dig into documentation and theology to find the truth. God had provided me with the perfect education, training, and experience to investigate the 2000 years of Jesus to separate fact from fiction, and after my NDE, I accepted the job. Now, nearly six years after the start of the most complex investigation I have ever conducted, I am providing the results. In summary, my goal for this investigation was to separate CRL theology from eyewitness testimony presented in the Bible to provide a complete evidence package that proves the story of Jesus to be true.

2

Investigation Support from the Expert

THROUGHOUT MY CAREER OF conducting various investigations, I relied on experts to provide feedback and advice to help guide and direct me to the truth. CRLs were trained in theology, and I had heard and studied most of their theology and written it off as fiction because it couldn't be proven with solid evidence. I was after evidence, and although at first it seemed as though I would be working alone on this investigation, I quickly realized that I was going to have the ultimate expert help from the Holy Spirit of God.

Several weeks after I started jotting down the words of Jesus from the Gospels and examining them, I began waking up with my head packed full of information that I had to write down and review. In addition, not long after that, I frequently woke up with dreams that caused me to lie in bed and ponder their meaning. My wife wondered if it was the effects of the stroke, but I knew my life had changed, and God was with me because having dreams was a new experience for me. I was in my 60s and throughout my life could only remember having a few dreams prior to the frequent ones I started having.

I quickly realized that the dreams were specific and intentional. Through them, I was getting directions for what Bible content to read in addition to guidance to help me understand the messages of what I was reading. In summary, I had hundreds of visions that provided guidance and direction over the nearly six-year investigation. I recorded many of these dreams because I either didn't immediately understand them and wanted to continue to review them, or the message was so important that I wanted frequent reminding of it.

For example, I documented the following visions:

- January 25, 2022: I woke up with the thought I needed to turn to the book of Revelation.
- February 1, 2022: I woke up with the Spirit telling me that I needed to do a comparison between Daniel and Revelation, just like I did with the Gospel writers.

I needed frequent reminders to start reviewing Daniel and Revelation prophecy because I didn't want to review them. I had studied Daniel and Revelation prophecy numerous times in the past, and they never made sense, so I didn't want to try again. In addition, I was investigating the word of God and searching for the truth about Jesus and CRL theology, so I didn't see how reviewing prophecy would help.

I disobeyed God's command and studied other material, then one day, soon after my rejection, God took an action to 'take away' my working computer. That event 'prompted' me to follow the Holy Spirit's direction, and I started reading Daniel's prophecy. For the first time, I started to connect Daniel to Jesus. Soon after, I reviewed my past dreams that I didn't understand, and I found one that now made perfect sense. God had provided me a vision that told me in advance I would initially reject his command to review prophecy. I chuckled at how thoroughly God knew me and could predict my behavior. Through these dreams and words that I was waking up with, I was amazed at how intricately involved God was in this investigation process.

Initially, I didn't understand what I was looking for in prophecy or why God had sent me there. I prayed and received the following guidance:

- February 7, 2022: I woke up this morning with the Spirit telling me that the book of Revelation is not about the end of the world; it is only about the Church. Focus on this, and my answers to what I am to do next will come.

If you have listened to CRL Revelation theology, the message God provided me is a huge shocker. CRLs claim that most of the prophecy in Revelation is all about the end time, with descriptions of the appearance of an Antichrist, the Rapture of the church, and a terrible seven-year Great Tribulation (ART) that includes a second coming of Jesus. That simple vision told me that Revelation does not support their widely accepted theology, which I refer to as ART because it is creative.

It was through that simple message in that dream that I started to understand God's message presented in prophecy. The learning process was steep, and there were roadblocks along the way, but I persevered. I tried to connect the New Covenant of Jesus (NC) church to Revelation and Daniel, but the pieces weren't always fitting together. After running into a brick wall time and time again, I resorted to prayer for help and in response, I received additional guidance and direction. One short but extremely valuable dream that helped was the following:

- July 1, 2022: I was told in this vision to continue with the book of Revelation, but be careful not to skip any verses.

Those who attempt to interpret the word of God often claim that a person must be flexible. Many experts believe they have a better understanding of the messages in the Bible if they are fluent in Greek or Hebrew. This is not at all the guidance I received from the Holy Spirit. I was told that to understand prophecy, I had to follow the story as it was being unfolded and focus on every word presented. Once I understood that every word in every verse in prophecy had meaning, I found it to have a chronological timeline element.

Then I ran into the math problem God provided in Daniel and Revelation, and it frustrated me because I couldn't solve it. There are numerous numbers presented in Daniel and Revelation that seemed to be connected (e.g., 7, 1260, 1290, 1335, 2300, and even "a time, times, and half a time), but I was unable to solve it. I kept at it for several weeks without success as I kept praying, then I received the following response:

- July 23, 2022: In my vision this morning, I am relearning calculus for some reason.

That dream might not seem like much to you, but it thoroughly explained what was about to happen. I immediately knew that the Holy Spirit had referred me back to the days when I first started studying calculus. In the early 1980s, I sat in a calculus class for three days trying to understand it. It was unusual for me not to immediately grasp a mathematical concept, and I was frustrated. On that third day, it was as though a flash bulb sparked in my head, and I immediately understood. The dream was telling me not to give up—keep on persevering, and like a flash, the meaning of the prophecy numbers will come to me. Several days later, that's exactly what happened. God knew about my trouble with calculus and connected it to understanding prophecy!

To understand prophecy, you will need to understand that it is ALL about the NC church of Jesus Christ. In addition, know that every word and verse is important, so don't skip any, understand that it has a chronological aspect to it, and never give up or create theology. Only then, if you persevere, the meaning will come to you in a flash like it did for me.

It is through prophecy that most of the details of Jesus' evidence package are revealed and proven to have been fulfilled. God ensured that I understood just how important prophecy is to the story of Jesus and how it is history told in advance by providing me with personal examples. For example, I had a dream on July 27, 2023, that my wife would get cancer. Since that time, she has had skin cancer detected and removed twice—first on October 17, 2023, and then on June 11, 2025. On March 26, 2023, I was shocked by a dream that abruptly woke me up, telling me that I had two tumors. On April 16, 2025, I was diagnosed with two tumors. God oversees the future and knows what will happen—this is the message I was getting that applied to my review of Daniel and Revelation prophecy. The documentation in those books may be considered prophecy, but it is more than that—they are God's evidence presented in advance.

God proved beyond a doubt that he knows the future through a sequence of dreams that directed my wife and me to where we were to live. On April 21, 2022, I had a dream to sell our home, and in that dream was a picture of an agent we had met several months before, but hadn't been in contact with her since. My wife was hesitant to move, but then that same morning, she received a text from that agent with a question: "Are you ready to sit down and discuss plans?" We called her up and told her about the dream matching the text she wrote, and she stated, "God has a plan." We sold, and God blessed us through this move that helped me with my stroke recovery.

Our move was to a condo across the street from the Atlantic Ocean beach. The stunning views of the sunrises, sunsets, and beach scenery motivated me to continue to investigate and write as I witnessed God's creation every day. After a little less than a year in the condo, I received the following dream, but note that I changed the names of the people in the dream to protect their identity:

> February 2023: Someone from work died whom I hardly knew, and someone was collecting money on their behalf. His last name

> was "Billford" or something like that. I asked how much people were contributing, and he said $20. I kept going in my pocket, which was full of bills, and pulling out a bill. I pulled out a seven and a three, then finally found a twenty and gave it to him. I hurried home to find three people, whom I thought were kids, standing on a chimney hooking up to an antenna. There were hazards all around the chimney—it was so small that they had to keep their balance, and there were live electrical wires above them. I was worried about them getting electrocuted.

This vision, like some of the others, presented a puzzle I needed to solve. I pondered the meaning of this vision and even sent my sister an email on July 24, 2023, telling her that I thought it might apply to a person in our family. Then, a few days later, July 26 and 27, I had back-to-back dreams about moving and cancer.

I continued to ponder the visions along with others I hadn't yet understood. Then, about a year after the "Billford" vision, my wife, who doesn't get visions like me but gets "gut feelings" to take certain actions, informed me that it was time to move. Somewhat reluctantly, I followed her 'guidance' to put our condo up for sale in January 2024, then we started shopping for a house about 150 miles inland to avoid hurricanes. In April 2024, we found a home that seemed perfect and made an offer contingent on the sale of our condo, which was accepted.

Of the dozen or more house closing processes we've been through, this one was by far the most difficult. But each of the numerous obstacles we encountered seemed to unexpectedly resolve. In May 2024, we finally had a firm closing agreement and date, so the owner provided a summary of utility and home service contacts and contracts. I took a quick look at that sheet, and my jaw dropped because the name of the lawn care service provider was "Billford." I knew right away that this very unusual last name was an exact match with the unusual name documented in the vision I had received in February 2023.

There was no way this was a coincidence, but I had no idea what the connection was to my dream. Of course, there are no $7 and $3 bills, so I knew this vision wasn't about the specified money. But regardless, for some reason, God had connected that earlier vision to the house we purchased more than a year later, and the connection hit me like a bolt of lightning.

Once we took possession of the home, I met Lonnie Billford, the lawn care contractor. A few weeks later, on July 27, 2024, I described the vision that was somehow connected to him. Lonnie gave me a strange look, then he explained the following, which I documented because it was so cool:

> His wife, Melissa Billford, experienced heart failure on March 4, 2023—about a week after I received my vision. Her heart stopped three times during the event, and she had to be shocked seven times to keep her alive. They have one child, so there are three of them in their family.

The electrical wire hazard in my vision corresponded to the electrical shocks that were necessary to save Melissa Billford's life. The seven-dollar bill represented the number of times the electrical shocks were administered to her, and the three-dollar bill was the number of times she was brought back to life. The three children on the roof underneath the electrical wires represented the three who most wanted her to live—Melissa, her husband Lonnie, and their one child. They are children of God!

There is another very interesting aspect to this vision. Later in this investigation, I will explain the Daniel 9:24–27 prophecy, commonly referred to as the "seventy sevens." A "seven" in Revelation prophecy is a reference to something that is perfect and complete. When the seven of prophecy is applied to the Billford event and circumstances, what happened to the Billfords is perfect and complete evidence provided by God to prove his power over life, death, and the future. In my vision, Melissa had to be shocked "seven" times to keep her alive. Her heart failure occurred on March 4, which is 03–4, and this adds up to "seven." The year of this event was 2023, which also adds up to another "seven." Together, the details of this event are 7-7-7, and this is no coincidence.

Every detail of this prophecy that has proven to be true can be supported with evidence. There is no doubt that God knew my future and predicted it. The message for you and me is related to the extensive amount of information I am required to obtain from prophecy to provide Jesus' evidence package. Prophecy is not words written that may or may not come true, and we are never to understand. Prophecy was written to provide exact details of what the future of the NC would look like. Prophecy is hard evidence because it came from God, and we know it happened.

As I go through prophecy, if you truly want to understand it, forget the theology you've been taught—in fact, block it out of your mind. Then, repeated here for emphasis, keep in mind the following:

- Understand that it is ALL about the NC,

- Every word and verse is important, so don't skip any,
- There is a chronological aspect to it, and,
- Pray and persevere until, like a flash, the meaning comes to you.

3

The Word of God

THROUGH EVENTS IN MY life and dreams that came true, God proved to me that he was a God of solid evidence. But when it came to Jesus being God, it was a bit of a mixed bag. I expected a solid evidence package from God proving to me that Jesus was the path to salvation, but I couldn't locate it. In summary, CRLs present a theological package consisting of the following claims to prove Jesus:

1. The Gospels are anonymous stories of a passed-down tradition that were documented many years after Jesus ascended back into heaven.
2. The names of the authors—Matthew, Mark, Luke, and John were provided by a group of men referred to as the 'early church fathers' (ECFs) who never met the disciples nor Jesus, but their claims are nearly unanimously accepted and confirmed in every Bible.
3. The Bible is in its entirety stated to be the infallible and inerrant word of God.

Passed-down stories of tradition are not testimony. Anonymous books are not testimony. Names of authors coming from ECFs that debated the origins of the Gospels to conclude that those men wrote them is not evidence. Stating that the Bible is the infallible and inerrant word of God is a circular argument used by other faiths. For example, Muslim religious leaders claim the word of God came through the word that was written by God in the Qur'an through their prophet Muhammad. The Mormons claim their founder, Joseph Smith, wrote the word of God in the Book of Mormon. I could present more, but claiming that a book was written by God, so every word in it must be from God, is not evidence. In summary, the package assembled by CRLs to tell the story of Jesus is not an evidence package that proves Jesus as God; it is a theological package that isn't backed by evidence.

A thorough search for additional Jesus' documentation within 100 years or so of Jesus' execution had me convinced that the Bible was my only reliable source of Jesus' documentation. Therefore, the sole source of possible evidence for the story of Jesus to be true is presented in the Christian Bible.

Every investigation I've carried out in the past started with defining the requirements. Manufacturing has specifications that need to be met, operations have procedures that need to be followed, and environmental, health, and safety aspects of work follow laws and standards. Certainly, God provided the world with specific requirements to be able to determine if the story of Jesus was also true. The fundamental foundation for Jesus presented in the Bible is that the word of God came through Jesus. CRLs believe this, and so do followers of Jesus. I expect that in the Bible, God provided clear guidance for who can speak for him; otherwise, everyone can claim it.

Starting with Jesus, he clearly claimed that he spoke for God:

> "For he whom God has sent speaks the words of God; for God gives the Spirit without measure." (John 3:34)

> "For I spoke not from myself, but the Father who sent me, he gave me a commandment, what I should say, and what I should speak. I know that his commandment is eternal life. The things I speak, even as the Father has said to me, so I speak." (John 12:49–50)

> "He who doesn't love me doesn't keep my words. The word which you hear isn't mine, but the Father's who sent me." (John 14:24)

Jesus stated that God "sent" him to speak for God. Jesus also claimed that God commanded him the words that he must speak. Very clearly, Jesus stated that his words came from God, whom he referred to as his Father.

But then Jesus went beyond claiming that God was his Father; he told the world that he and God were equals:

> "I and the Father are one." (John 10:30)

Jesus stated that his words came from God because he IS God. Jesus also described his words as having power that could only come from God:

> "Most certainly I tell you, he who hears my word and believes him who sent me has eternal life, and doesn't come into judgment, but has passed out of death into life." (John 5:24)

> "Most certainly, I tell you, if a person keeps my word, he will never see death." (John 8:51)

Only God can judge the dead and promise eternal life, and Jesus stated that those who hear his words and follow them will not be judged and they "will never see death." With this as a starting point, there is no doubt that the words of Jesus are stated in the Bible to be the word of God.

Jesus also validated the words of Moses as the word of God. Jesus healed a leper, then said to him:

> "See that you say nothing to anybody, but go show yourself to the priest and offer for your cleansing the things which Moses commanded, for a testimony to them." (Mark 1:44)

Jesus told the healed leper to testify to the religious leaders in accordance with Moses' commands. Jesus, as God, healed a man and then commanded him to follow the Law of Moses, indicating that the Law of Moses came from God. Jesus also referenced miracles documented by Moses and connected the miracles to the promise of the dead having eternal life:

> "But about the dead, that they are raised, haven't you read in the book of Moses about the bush, how God spoke to him, saying, 'I am the God of Abraham, the God of Isaac, and the God of Jacob'?" (Mark 12:26)

Jesus referred to the "scriptures" (Mark 12:24) and then connected God's gift of eternal life and miracles to the "book of Moses." God's appearance to Moses in the burning bush was Moses' introduction to God—the first miracle in his life that he recorded. Many more miracles of God through Moses were recorded after the burning bush. Jesus, as God, has just validated Moses' book as coming from God. Therefore, Moses' books are the word of God.

We also find that Jesus used words from the "book of Moses" to prove himself to be God:

> God said to Moses, "I AM WHO I AM," and he said, "You shall tell the children of Israel this: I AM has sent me to you." (Exodus 3:14)

> Jesus said to them, "Most certainly, I tell you, before Abraham came into existence, I AM." (John 8:58)

Moses wrote that in the burning bush, God described himself as "I AM." Jesus used this reference to claim that he was the same as the God who spoke to Moses. There can be no doubt that the evidence proves Jesus endorsed the words of Moses to be the word of God.

Several verses in the book of Moses—the first five books in the Bible that are also referred to as the "Law," "Hebrew Torah," or "Pentateuch," are interpreted to predict a future Messiah. Some very important prophecy verses written by Moses include Genesis 3:15, 22:18, 49:10, Numbers 24:17, and the following:

> [18] I will raise them up a prophet from among their brothers, like you. I will put my words in his mouth, and he shall speak to them all that I shall command him. [19] It shall happen that whoever will not listen to my words which he shall speak in my name, I will require it of him. (Deuteronomy 18:18–19)

Moses prophesied a specific future prophet who would come and speak for God. This prophet, who is referred to as a Messiah, will have authority over men and women because God WILL REQUIRE the words of the Messiah to be listened to—the Messiah will be a ruler. God will require ALL to listen to the Messiah, even if they don't want to listen—in other words, there will be a penalty for those who reject the Messiah.

Not only did Moses prophecy the future Messiah, but many other OT prophets did too. For example, some of them include the following:

- Isaiah 7:14—from the house of David, "the virgin will conceive, and bear a son, and shall call his name Immanuel" (Matthew 1:18–23)
- Micah 5:2—"But you, Bethlehem Ephrathah, being small among the clans of Judah, out of you one will come out to me that is to be the ruler in Israel" (Matthew 2:1)
- Zechariah 12:10—"I will pour on David's house, and on the inhabitants of Jerusalem, the spirit of grace and of supplication, and they will look to me, whom they have pierced; and they shall mourn for him, as one mourns for his only son, and will grieve bitterly for him, as one grieves for his firstborn." (John 19:34–37)

- Hosea 11:1—"When Israel was a child, then I loved him, and called my son out of Egypt." (Matthew 2:13–15)
- Psalm 22:18 [David]—"They divide my garments among them. They cast lost for my clothing." (John 19:23–24)
- Malachi 3:1—"Behold, I send my messenger, and he will prepare the way before me; and the Lord, whom you seek, will suddenly come to his temple; and the messenger of the covenant, whom you desire, behold, he comes!" says Yahweh of Armies. (Matthew 11:4–10)

This list is not all-inclusive because there are other OT prophets who also prophesied the Messiah.

Jesus claimed to be the prophesied Messiah and ruler:

> [25] The woman said to him, "I know that Messiah is coming, he who is called Christ. When he has come, he will declare to us all things." [26] Jesus said to her, "I am he, the one who speaks to you." (John 4:25–26)

Jesus affirmed that he fulfilled the role of the promised Messiah. Jesus also explained his role as the Messiah:

> "Don't think that I came to destroy the law or the prophets. I didn't come to destroy, but to fulfill." (Matthew 5:17)

> "But all this has happened that the Scriptures of the prophets might be fulfilled." Then all the disciples left him and fled. (Matthew 26:56)

Jesus DID NOT come to destroy or replace the words of the OT prophets; he came to fulfil them. Moses and the OT Prophets predicted a Messiah from God, and Jesus stated he fulfilled that prophecy.

With the following words, Jesus again validated the words of Moses, whom the Jews believed to have come from God and claimed that he fulfilled the Messiah prophecy written by Moses:

> "For if you believed Moses, you would believe me; for he wrote about me." (John 5:46)

Jesus stated he was the Messiah, and his words as the word of God are to be believed and followed. Since Jesus spoke for God, Moses also spoke for God and MUST be believed. Taking that one step further, the OT prophets who also prophesied about Jesus are to be believed because their words came from God.

Moses recorded in his book specific criteria from God that must be used to separate false teachers from prophets sent by God to speak for Him:

> [20] But the prophet who speaks a word presumptuously in my name, which I have not commanded him to speak, or who speaks in the name of other gods, that same prophet shall die." You may say in your heart, "How shall we know the word which Yahweh has not spoken?" When a prophet speaks in Yahweh's name, if the thing doesn't follow, nor happen, that is the thing which Yahweh has not spoken. The prophet has spoken it presumptuously. You shall not be afraid of him. (Deuteronomy 18:20–22)

For a prophet to be from God, two things must happen: they must predict the Messiah, and their predictions MUST come true. If either one fails to happen, a prophet did not come from God, so "You shall not be afraid of him." Jesus claimed to be the Messiah and, through his transfiguration event, in which Moses and Elijah appeared alive with him (Mark 9:2–8), he proved that OT prophets were from God and that they have eternal life.

However, note that if Jesus is not proven to be the Messiah, then "the thing" has not yet happened, and all the OT prophets are yet to be proven to have spoken for God. In other words, we have a circular argument of the OT prophets pointing to Jesus and Jesus claiming that he met the OT prophet criteria to be the one they predicted. The whole truth of the Bible story of the OT prophets through Jesus hinges on evidence that proves the story of Jesus to be true. If Jesus cannot be proven as the Messiah, those who predicted "the thing" are wrong and were not from God, at least until a proven Messiah appears later.

Before moving on, consider the NT contents to compare the words in it to what is specified to be the word of God in Deuteronomy. Assuming the evidence package will prove Jesus as the Messiah and God, certainly the OT prophets who predicted Jesus are proven to have spoken for God. In addition, Jesus' words as God are proven to be the word of God. But what about Paul's thirteen letters and the book of Acts and other letters from anonymous/unidentified authors (Hebrews, Jude, and James)? If you follow God's law specified in Deuteronomy by Moses, who was authorized to speak for God, those are not the word of God because they aren't prophecy about Jesus. The words of Jesus and the words of the OT prophets are the word of God, but all that other material in the Bible doesn't meet God's requirements.

Consider this conclusion carefully, because I haven't added or deleted requirements; I'm providing them from the Bible. CRLs have assembled a package of documents and called it the Bible, then they created theology that claims the Bible is the inherent and infallible word of God. But, according to the word of God, those additions to the Bible ARE NOT the word of God and don't belong there. We have a discrepancy between what the CRLs are teaching throughout the world and what is written in the Law. We will revisit this subject again as we proceed through the investigation.

In summary, through Deuteronomy, God specified who could speak for him. Only the words of the Messiah sent by God and the OT prophets who predicted the Messiah meet Deuteronomy Law requirements for being able to speak for God. CRLs have created a theology that states the Bible is the inerrant and infallible word of God, and this allows them to teach followers of Jesus that the words of Paul and others are the word of God. Atheists love to point to these facts as a circular argument for attempting to disprove Christianity, and they have a point.

However, the words in Deuteronomy will be proven to be the word of God ONLY if Jesus is proven to be the Messiah. The word of God through Jesus and the OT prophets hinges on having solid evidence to prove Jesus as the Messiah.

4

God Defines and Jesus Confirms the Evidence Requirements

TOGETHER, THE WORDS OF Moses and Jesus presented in the Bible present a clear definition of who God authorized to speak for him. But I have never met Moses nor Jesus, so how can I prove that what is written by them came from God? I expect solid evidence because God provided me proof of his existence through miracles in my life. God also provided me a vision of the Spirit of a friend who had just died and was at peace with Jesus. Finally, God also provided me evidence that there is hell for those who reject or doubt Jesus. Based on this, I expect clear evidence from God to prove that the words of Moses and Jesus written in the Bible are from God.

After a bit of research, I found words of Moses that described to me what the expected evidence is to look like:

> At the mouth of two witnesses, or three witnesses, he who is to die shall be put to death. At the mouth of one witness, he shall not be put to death. (Deuteronomy 17:6)

> One witness shall not rise up against a man for any iniquity, or for any sin that he sins. At the mouth of two witnesses, or at the mouth of three witnesses, shall a matter be established. (Deuteronomy 19:15)

Let me start by saying that God's criteria for proving a matter are expected and make sense. I have interviewed and interrogated witnesses for many years and understand the importance of their testimony. I also understand how testimony must be screened and analyzed to determine its truthfulness. Throughout my professional career, witness testimony is only valid when coming from observers. Second-hand or worse statements can sometimes help to find the truth by providing leads, but they cannot determine the truthfulness of a matter because it is unreliable.

There is no matter more serious than one that determines the life or death of a person. Believing in Jesus is an eternal life-or-death matter according to the words of Moses, the OT Prophets, and Jesus. Belief in Jesus is the most important matter of a person's life, and the passed-down oral tradition-based Gospels written years after Jesus' sacrifice do not meet God's requirements in Deuteronomy or even current standards. According to what Moses wrote, his prophecy for the Messiah came from God only if Jesus is proven to be the Messiah. According to the Law, we need two or three witnesses to prove Jesus is God the Messiah, or the whole Christian faith falls apart for lack of evidence. In summary, the eyewitness testimony to prove Jesus as God and the Messiah must meet the highest standard.

Jesus didn't shy away from the Deuteronomy Law testimony requirement; he confirmed it. He wanted his words and miracles to be held to the highest testimony standards of Deuteronomy Law. Jesus was recorded discussing the testimony evidence requirement three times in the Gospel of John. First, Jesus discussed it with a group of Jews:

> "If I testify about myself, my witness is not valid." (John 5:31)

Jesus made it very clear that following the Deuteronomy Law evidence requirement to prove him as the Messiah IS GOD'S COMMAND that is to be followed. Jesus knew that eyewitness testimony from others was needed to prove himself as the Messiah and God. After Jesus made this point, he listed John the Baptist (JB) as one of his witnesses (John 5:32). Then Jesus claimed God as his witness:

> "But the testimony which I receive is not from man. However, I say these things that you may be saved." (John 5:34)

Jesus stated that he met the requirements of Deuteronomy through evidence presented by eyewitnesses and therefore must be believed. But the religious leaders rejected his evidence (John 5:35–47). They didn't agree that God had testified on behalf of Jesus, even though Jesus had performed miraculous works, just as Moses did, that were witnessed and testified to (e.g., Mark 3:1–5 and others).

Second, religious leaders confronted Jesus about the evidence requirement to prove himself as the Messiah:

> The Pharisees, therefore, said to him, "You testify about yourself. Your testimony is not valid." (John 8:13)

They knew that according to the Law of Moses provided by God, two or three witnesses were required. In response, Jesus lectured the religious leaders because he knew no amount of evidence would convince them of the truth (John 8:14–16). I encounter the same issue when discussing evidence requirements with God-hating self-proclaimed atheists who reject evidence without even evaluating it.

Then Jesus reminded the religious leaders of the Law they claimed to be upholding, but in fact were ignoring and rejecting:

> [17] It's also written in your law that the testimony of two people is valid. [18] I am one who testifies about myself, and the Father who sent me testifies about me." (John 8:17–18)

Again, Jesus affirmed that he met the evidence requirement—even without the testimony of JB, who had likely been executed by this time. The religious leaders rejected this testimony again and even referred to Jesus as a "demon" (John 8:19–56). Then, by referring to the "I AM" words God used to describe himself to Moses, Jesus claimed he was God (John 8:58). In response, the religious leaders demonstrated their rejection of the evidence proving Jesus as God by picking up stones to kill him. But Jesus' decreed sacrifice time had not yet come (John 8:59), so he left unharmed.

Then later in the Gospel of John, there is a third reference to God's Law for requiring eyewitness testimony to prove Jesus as the Messiah:

> The Jews therefore came around him and said to him, "How long will you hold us in suspense? If you are the Christ, tell us plainly." Jesus answered them, "I told you, and you don't believe. The works that I do in my Father's name, these testify about me." (John 10:24–25)

Jesus referenced additional evidence to support his fulfilment of the Law witness requirement. Jesus performed numerous "works" throughout his ministry, and he stated, rightfully so, that his miracles were proof that God was testifying for him. After this third recorded testimony discussion in John, the religious leaders again picked up stones to kill Jesus (John 10:31–38). Just as before, the decreed time of Jesus' sacrifice had not yet come, so he again escaped unharmed (John 10:39). You know the rest of the story—ultimately, the religious leaders rejected Jesus and had him executed. But this was God's plan all along—to have Jesus sacrificed for the removal of sin from believers.

Anyone can claim God as their witness, but it takes evidence to support it. The numerous miracles that Moses performed in the name of God were proof to those of Moses' generation that God was with Moses. Likewise, the miracles that Jesus performed, as documented in the Gospels, were proof to the people who witnessed them that God was a witness for Jesus. Jesus and Moses both PERFORMED miracles to prove that God was with them. The religious leaders of Jesus' time who rejected him had either witnessed Jesus' miracles or had access to witnesses who did. They had the testimony and evidence they needed to validate Jesus through Moses' words, but they rejected it.

But what about the generations outside of Moses, the OT prophets, and Jesus' time? They have not seen the miracles, nor have they had physical access to witnesses who did. This is also a fact for me and you, as we haven't witnessed the miracles of Moses and Jesus. In summary, Jesus as the Messiah is the most important matter in the history of the world and testimony of his miracles proving him to be God is expected. But the Gospels that describe the miracles of Jesus are presented as handed-down accounts written by ECF claimed authors rather than proven eyewitness testimonies.

Hopefully, you now understand the dilemma facing those searching for the true word of God. The Bible says not to believe in Jesus unless there are two or three witnesses to validate Jesus as the Messiah and God, and the CRLs present us with theology instead of eyewitness testimony. In summary, the only possible path available for Christians to believe in Jesus is through the CRL theology package, but to do this, followers of Jesus are ignoring God's testimony requirements.

Something is drastically wrong because the God I know in my life would never leave this theological mess to prove Jesus. We can be certain that the evidence package for Jesus was presented, but it is missing. You can now understand why God presented me with the NDE to get me to work. My job is to find out what happened to the evidence package for Jesus and present it!

5

The Evidence Package and a Theology Warning

THE DETAILS OF THE evidence package for Jesus are found embedded in prophecy presented in the Olivet Discourse. If you have been a student of CRL theology, you are likely scratching your head because CRLs near unanimously claim that the Olivet Discourse is prophecy supporting ART theology. As noted earlier, CRL ART theology describes a seven-year period when a powerful antichrist appears and the Christian rapture, great tribulation, and Jesus' second coming all occur. CRLs also claim that, along with the Olivet Discourse, Daniel and Revelation prophecy support their ART theology.

Remember that Billford dream that told me about a year in advance, where I would be moving to? That dream was evidence that God knows the future and can tell the world about it prior to it taking place. In other words, prophecy is not a 'prediction' of what might happen in the future; it is evidence of the future provided in advance. Prophecy in the Olivet Discourse, Daniel, and Revelation are solid evidence proving Jesus to the world because there is no doubt that what was presented in them by God occurred. Through prophecy, God provided the details of the evidence package that Jesus presented AND described all the details of what happened to it.

As stated already, you will find the details of Jesus' evidence package embedded in the Olivet Discourse. But to get to those details, I must first 'deprogram' you. The reason I must deprogram you is that you have been repeatedly told that the Olivet Discourse is not an evidence package for Jesus; it is telling you about end-time ART theology. You can only find and understand the evidence package for Jesus and know what happened to it by blocking ART theology out of your mind. I know this for a fact because even though I was skeptical of ART theology from the first time I heard it, for a time, the memory of it impeded me from understanding the word of God presented in prophecy.

Starting with the theology of ART from an article titled, "What is the Olivet Discourse?" accessed on July 13, 2025, from the website https://www.gotquestions.org/Olivet-discourse.html, typical CRL end times theology is introduced by GotQuestions.org:

> "His subject is the end times. This discourse is recorded in Matthew 24:1—25:46."

> "The record in Matthew is the most extensive, so reference here will be to Matthew's Gospel."

According to CRLs, the Olivet Discourse prophecy has nothing to do with Jesus' evidence package or what happened to it; it is all about the end time. Also note that "Matthew" is used to support their theology because they claim it "is the most extensive." That is a misleading statement.

Next, an explanation of end-time CRL theology connects the Olivet Discourse to the words of Paul, Daniel, and Revelation. From the following GotQuestions.org article titled, "What is going to happen according to end time prophecy?" accessed at https://www.gotquestions.org/end-times.html, on July 13, 2025, are additional scripture references that CRLs claim support ART end time theology:

> "Christ will remove all born-again believers from the earth in. . .the rapture (1 Thessalonians 4:13–18; 1 Corinthians 15:51–54). At the judgment seat these believers will be rewarded. . .or will lose rewards, but not eternal life. . . (1 Corinthians 3:11–15; 2 Corinthians 5:10)."

> "The Antichrist (the beast) will come into power and will sign a covenant with Israel for seven years (Daniel 9:27) . . .known as the "tribulation."

> "About halfway through the seven years, the Antichrist will break the peace covenant with Israel and make war against it. The Antichrist will commit "the abomination of desolation" and set up an image of himself to be worshiped in the Jerusalem temple (Daniel 9:27; 2 Thessalonians 2:3–10) . . ."

> "The second half of the tribulation is known as 'the great tribulation' (Revelation 7:14) and 'the time of Jacob's trouble' (Jeremiah 30:7)."
>
> "Jesus Christ will return, destroy the Antichrist and his armies. . .cast them into the lake of fire (Revelation 19:11–21) . . .then bind Satan in the Abyss for 1,000 years and. . .rule His earthly kingdom for this thousand-year period (Revelation 20:1–6)."

In summary, the foundation for ART theology is based on the following Bible references:

1. The Olivet Discourse in Matthew,
2. Numerous references to the words of Paul from four separate letters—1 and 2 Corinthians and 1 and 2 Thessalonians,
3. Daniel 9:27,
4. Revelation 7:14 and 20:1–6, and,
5. Jeremiah 30:7

Considering them one at a time, the Olivet Discourse is provided in three Gospels, but Gotquestions.org claims they refer to the Matthew version because it "is the most extensive." Every CRL's discussion of the ART theology I've witnessed refers to the Matthew Olivet Discourse version, and it isn't because it's the most extensive; it's because it's the version that supports their ART theology.

Of the other two accounts of the Olivet Discourse, the Gospel of Mark provides a completely different message in that version of the Olivet Discourse, and it has nothing to do with ART. I will not consider the Gospel of Luke because the author of the Gospel of Luke admitted he was not providing a personal testimony of Jesus. There is a statement in Luke that the author carefully investigated the story of Jesus, but he didn't witness what he wrote about. Furthermore, he didn't provide the names of his sources, and he didn't name himself. In summary, the documentation in that book cannot be considered eyewitness testimony because we have no proof of who wrote the documentation or where it came from.

A comparison of a sampling of the Olivet Discourse accounts in Matthew and Mark explains why the Matthew version is the source for ART theology:

> "and then the sign of the Son of Man will appear in the sky. Then all the tribes of the earth will mourn, and they will see the Son of Man coming on the clouds of the sky with power and great glory." (Matthew 24:30)
>
> "At that time, people will see the Son of Man coming in clouds with great power and glory. (Mark 13:26)

The version in Matthew duplicates a good portion of Mark, but there are modifications to it. Matthew indicates that Jesus will be visible and everyone will see him, whereas the version in Mark indicates that Jesus won't be visible—he will be hidden "in clouds." Matthew's version claims that Jesus' return will be a physical appearance, and this is an important aspect of ART theology. Through ART, everyone watches and waits for the glorious appearance of Jesus. The description in Mark's verse doesn't meet that criterion; it describes Jesus in clouds, indicating that his return is symbolic or spiritual, rather than physical and visible.

The next verse also indicates that Matthew's author copied from Mark, with a few minor changes made:

> As he sat on the Mount of Olives, the disciples came to him privately (Matthew 24:3)
>
> As Jesus was sitting on the Mount of Olives opposite the temple, Peter, James, John and Andrew asked him privately, (Mark 13:3)

As I continue through this book, you will find it common for Matthew's author to have copied from Mark and left off eyewitness details. There are two reasons for the accounts to differ. First, the false teachers edited the copied material in Matthew to make it appear as though it was the eyewitness Matthew witnessing the same event. The second reason for the accounts not being the same is that false teachers made edits to support their theft of the NC.

The edit to Matthew 24:3 is to support theology AND indicate that a disciple named Matthew witnessed Jesus describing the Olivet Discourse. First, Mark describes Jesus separating four disciples from the rest and "privately" providing them with this prophecy. Matthew is not included, so he is not a witness. However, in Matthew, Jesus takes "the disciples" and "privately" describes prophecy to them. The false teachers slipped up in their edits because they edited the copied event, but forgot to remove the "privately" description. In Matthew, Jesus did not take the disciples privately aside because he was already with them, and nobody else was described there.

In Mark, Jesus provides prophecy details of the future for four of his disciples. We can be certain of that because throughout Mark 13:5–14, Jesus is recorded as stating "you" at least twelve times to those four disciples. These references in the Mark version prove that Jesus is providing the prophecy of the future to THOSE FOUR DISCIPLES. Matthew supports end-time ART theology, Mark doesn't.

CRLs also twist the meaning of another verse to support their ART theology, as evidenced by the following:

> "Most certainly I tell you, this generation will not pass away until all these things are accomplished." (Matthew 24:34)

> "Most certainly I say to you, this generation will not pass away until all these things happen." (Mark 13:30)

Again, Matthew is a copy of what's presented in Mark, with some slight word manipulation to make it seem as though Matthew's author is witnessing this event. The message is clear in Mark that Jesus has taught four disciples about their future, then informed them that everything described in the Olivet Discourse will happen during their lifetimes. This doesn't fit end-time theology, so CRLs create theology to describe "this generation" in Matthew as a reference to the generation living at the end time, the second coming of Jesus. Jesus predicted the future of those four disciples, and every event he described in the Olivet Discourse will be witnessed by THEIR generation—unless you consider the Matthew version.

Next up for analysis are the words of Paul that CRLs claim support ART theology. Earlier, I presented the word of God that provided criteria for those who could speak for God and found that Paul's words did not meet God's criteria. Paul's words are not the word of God, so Paul cannot speak prophecy on behalf of God—it is forbidden by God's Laws in Deuteronomy. If Paul's words are used to support CRL ART theology, then that theology is not from God.

Then there is Daniel 9:27 that takes only one of the seventy-sevens of Daniel 9:24–27 out of context and extends it out to the end time. Daniel 9:24–27 is an answer to prayer about God redeeming Daniel's people, and it is all about Jesus, not the end times. What else would it address as an answer to the redemption of people in the future? As you will see later, Daniel 9:24–27 has nothing to do with the great tribulation component of

ART theology; it describes the exact and complete details of Jesus' arrival and mission.

ART prophecy also relies on a few sections of Revelation for support. CRLs claim that Revelation 7:14 is a reference to an end-time great tribulation, but Acts 8:1 describes the great persecution beginning with Stephen's stoning death. As you will see from the analysis of prophecy, the martyrs of chapter seven in Revelation, being referenced in 7:14, are those who were executed during the great tribulation that has already ended. You will find out too that there is no need to wait for the end time antichrist because he entered the NC at the beginning. Furthermore, Revelation 20:1–6 will connect to the martyrs of the great tribulation leading to the transition to the 1000-year reign of Jesus that we are currently in. But I am getting too far ahead of myself, as all this will be explained step-by-step in the following chapters.

There is also one additional verse used by CRLs to promote ART theology, Jeremiah 30:7, and I'm really scratching my head because I fail to see the connection between that one verse and ART theology. Now that I have you doubting the Olivet Discourse connection to ART theology, it's time to move forward to present the evidence package plan provided by Jesus in the Olivet Discourse that we can be assured was implemented.

6

Jesus Prepares the Evidence Package

LETTING GO OF ART theology and focusing solely on the words that Jesus spoke to James, John, Peter, and Andrew in the Olivet Discourse will lead you straight to the evidence trail for Jesus:

> [9] "But watch yourselves, for they will deliver you up to councils. You will be beaten in synagogues. You will stand before rulers and kings for my sake, for a testimony to them. [10] The Good News must first be preached to all the nations. [11] When they lead you away and deliver you up, don't be anxious beforehand or premeditate what you will say, but say whatever will be given you in that hour. For it is not you who speaks, but the Holy Spirit. (Mark 13:9–11)

There are three verses in this summary, and two of them describe the future persecution of these four disciples. Jesus stated that they will be arrested, beaten, and provide their testimony to rulers and kings (Mark 13:9). Jesus also stated "they [will] lead you away and deliver you up", which is certainly a reference to the execution of these four disciples (Mark 13:11).

Those four disciples will be arrested, persecuted, and then eventually killed. But then there is the following very important message sandwiched between Mark 13:9 and 13:11, repeated here for emphasis:

> The Good News must first be preached to all the nations. (Mark 13:10)

Hmmm. . .prior to the persecution and execution of these four disciples, a very important event "must" happen, "The Good News MUST FIRST be preached to all the nations." The Good News will not spread throughout the world by itself—somebody needs to do something, so this "MUST FIRST" statement to these four disciples is a command from Jesus.

Jesus is talking to the four disciples, and prior to them being persecuted and executed, the world MUST have the evidence package to prove Jesus to the world. There is only one way that this command through prophecy can be fulfilled: Jesus' eyewitnesses MUST provide their eyewitness testimony about Jesus in accordance with Deuteronomy 17:6 and 19:15. Their eyewitness testimony is to "be preached to ALL THE NATIONS" prior to their persecution and their deaths. Therefore, the testimony of these four eyewitnesses cannot be verbal; for this command to be fulfilled, it must be written.

The Gospels will come from Jesus' chosen eyewitnesses, James, John, Peter, and Andrew. Jesus provided us additional proof of his command to these four disciples. Eyewitnesses need to observe what they are testifying to. Jesus chose four eyewitnesses to provide their testimony, AND he made sure those four men observed everything Jesus did and said so that their testimony would be complete. Jesus had an 'inner circle' of disciples that he separated from the rest and took with him to witness everything. For example, the four disciples are documented as witnessing:

- The synagogue ruler's daughter was raised back to life from the dead (Mark 5:36–43)
- The transfiguration of Jesus, when he appeared with Moses and Elijah, proved that there is eternal life. (Mark 9:2–4)
- Prophecy of their future through the Olivet Discourse (Mark 13:1–37)
- Jesus preparing to make his decreed sacrifice (Mark 14:32–42)

Jesus taking these four disciples with him privately to observe everything Jesus did and said is an important piece of evidence validating them as Jesus' personally chosen eyewitnesses. But wait, if you are an astute student of the Bible, this is where you tell me that there were only three inner circle disciples because Andrew was not one of them. Andrew may not be listed as one, but the evidence in the Gospels indicates that Jesus certainly included him in the inner circle.

First and foremost, we know that Jesus appointed Andrew (Mark 13:3, 10) as one of his eyewitnesses; therefore, he MUST be in the inner circle too. Second, Andrew, who, with his friend John, witnessed JB point out Jesus as the Messiah, then left JB to follow Jesus (John 1:35–40). Andrew and John were Jesus' first two recorded disciples! Third, the first thing that Andrew did after he met Jesus was to go find his brother Peter and take him to meet Jesus, whom Andrew referred to as the Messiah (John 1:41). Andrew was the first disciple recorded to have recognized Jesus as the Messiah! Fourth, from the words of John, we learn that Andrew was a trusted leader of the disciples. John recorded that Philip, another one of the twelve disciples, had to go through Andrew to approach Jesus to introduce some Greeks to Jesus (John 12:21–22). This indicates that Andrew was what in modern-day terms is called a 'Chief of Staff.' Andrew was Jesus' right-hand man, and John became Jesus' deputy. The first two disciples who met Jesus were very important men involved in Jesus' mission.

What doesn't make sense is that Andrew, a man who Jesus appointed to provide his testimony (Mark 13:3), is not documented as one of Jesus' inner circle disciples and is rarely addressed in the Gospels. The author of Mark noted that Jesus went to the house where Peter and Andrew (Mark 1:29) lived to heal Peter's mother-in-law. Outside of that reference and him being listed as one of the twelve (Matthew 10:2 and Mark 3:18) and documented as being recruited with his brother Peter (Matthew 4:18 and Mark 1:12), Andrew is invisible. The absence of Andrew from the inner circle and in general from the Gospel is, to this fraud investigator, not accidental. Just as there was an issue with the omission of the four disciples from Matthew 24:3's copied version of Mark 13:3, and some additional edits to Matthew to hide the copying and make it seem like the author who copied was an eyewitness, Andrew being written out of the Gospels is indicative of fraud.

Recall that Jesus stated the Good News would be documented BEFORE the persecution of his eyewitnesses began. From this very important detail, we can determine WHEN the testimonies were documented. Acts 7:1–60 tells the story of the stoning death of Stephen. After that is the following verse defining the start of the great tribulation:

> A great persecution arose against the assembly which was in Jerusalem in that day. (Acts 8:1)

The "great persecution" of the disciples and followers of Jesus—the "assembly" or NC, began at the time of Stephen's execution. Most scholars reference the death of Stephen as having occurred between 33 and 35 AD. Jesus is estimated to have been sacrificed and resurrected in 30 AD. I don't want to continue providing the evidence package while referring to a three-year span from 33–35 AD for the start of the tribulation, when I know that evidence presented later will show the year of Stephen's stoning death to be 33 AD. For this reason, I will present the great tribulation starting on the day the testimonies of Jesus were completed, in 33 AD.

Thus far, through the words of the Bible, it is proven that Paul's words are not the word of God, Andrew was edited out of the Gospels, and the copied version of the Olivet Discourse in Matthew was edited to support ART theology. That's a fair amount of corruption already identified in the Christian package for proving the story of Jesus to be true. Knowing this, how can I be sure that the evidence package from the four eyewitnesses will be reliable testimony?

The answer is from the word of God—because Jesus assured it would be. In fact, Jesus promised that the testimony to prove him to all the people of the world would be the most accurate testimony ever provided in history:

> [25] "I have said these things to you while still living with you. [26] But the Counselor, the Holy Spirit, whom the Father will send in my name, will teach you all things, and will remind you of all that I said to you. (John 14:25–26)

The disciples would not have to rely solely on their memories to get the details perfect, because Jesus promised to send them the Holy Spirit to explain everything and remind them of all the details. The Holy Spirit was promised to the disciples so that they would document the message of Jesus perfectly and completely—just the way God commanded it to be. God would be involved, so their testimonies couldn't get any more accurate than that.

Memories of people fade over time, so the sooner testimony is recorded after an event, the more reliable it is. Since the reliability of eyewitness testimony is affected by the passing of time, I expect Jesus to have addressed this, too. Through the following, we obtain the official start date:

> [21] Jesus therefore said to them again, "Peace be to you. As the Father has sent me, even so I send you." [22] When he had said this, he breathed on them and said to them, "Receive the Holy Spirit! (John 20:21–22)

Jesus appeared to his disciples on the first day of his resurrection and breathed the promised Holy Spirit into them. Not only do we have the exact day the Gospels were completed—the day Stephen was stoned to death, but we also have the exact day the disciples started working on them. Jesus provided you with the exact period for the testimony to be documented.

There is only one additional consideration to ensure the testimonies of Jesus are reliable—their preservation over time. CRLs claim we have passed down stories of tradition, and this is a quality of unreliable testimony. Jesus promised the opposite:

> Heaven and earth will pass away, but my words will not pass away. (Mark 13:31)

With a promise from Jesus that his words will last forever, we can be assured that what we are reading today is exactly what Jesus' eyewitnesses documented. How did this happen? God was in control of translations and preservation of the Gospel through the years. God protected the Gospels for nearly 2000 years to ensure their integrity.

Verbal testimony CANNOT satisfy Mark 13:31 because testimony becomes more and more unreliable as it is passed from person to person. The Bible may not be in its entirety the inerrant and infallible word of God, but we can be assured that it contains it. Jesus made sure that those four disciples observed everything that he did and spoke. Then on the first day of his resurrection, Jesus breathed the Holy Spirit into them so that they could immediately get started on documenting every detail of Jesus that God wanted shared with the world. The disciples were reminded of their observations, and they wrote them down between 30 and 33 AD to ensure the people of all nations and languages would have reliable testimonies of Jesus. Jesus also assured future generations could trust that they were reading the unaltered words of Jesus in their testimonies because his words would outlive heaven and the earth. The commentary of the eyewitnesses may have been altered by false teachers, but the words of Jesus have not been changed—they were recorded exactly as spoken and are the same today as the day they were written by Jesus' eyewitnesses.

7

Corruption of the Evidence Package

WHAT HAPPENED AFTER THE disciples presented their testimony to the world is described through two words: corruption and fraud. How do we know? First, in the Olivet Discourse, Jesus warned that Satan was determined to destroy the NC:

> Jesus, answering, began to tell them, "Be careful that no one leads you astray. For many will come in my name, saying, 'I am he!' and will lead many astray." (Mark 13:5–6)

Jesus warned about evil affecting both the disciples and followers of Jesus. When I first read this verse, I wondered how the disciples could be led astray by false teachers. The concept of the disciples being persuaded to abandon Jesus to follow the words of false teachers didn't seem possible.

Then I read the following words written by John, and I understood Jesus' warning:

> Dear children, this is the last hour, and as you have heard that the antichrist is coming, even now many antichrists have come. This is how we know it is the last hour. They went out from us, but they did not really belong to us. For if they had belonged to us, they would have remained with us; but their going showed that none of them belonged to us. (1 John 2:18–19)

Jesus hadn't warned the disciples about losing their faith in him; Jesus warned them about being betrayed by persuasive false teachers whom they had chosen as their successors. John and the other eyewitnesses shared their testimony to follow Jesus' command to spread the Good News throughout the nations. John stated that they chose and trained leaders to help spread the Good News, then "They went out from us." John didn't state that some of the men the disciples chose to succeed them were loyal to the disciples. John didn't state that one or even a few false teachers infiltrated the ranks of the disciples. John stated that "none of them belonged to us." John belonged to Jesus, so the antichrists who were taking over the NC were not followers of Jesus; they were false teachers who had led the disciples astray. John stated that he was witnessing a false teacher NC coup.

There is another very important concept in that summary by John. Note that he stated, "This is how we know it is the last hour," indicating that the NC will last one hour, and it will be the final time for people on the earth. It sounds weird unless you consider the "hour" to be a reference to the 'eternity clock.' Jesus also validated the NC as being an hour long:

> Jesus said to her, "Woman, what does that have to do with you and me? My hour has not yet come." (John 2:4)

> Jesus said to her, "Woman, believe me, the hour is coming when neither in this mountain nor in Jerusalem will you worship the Father. (John 4:21)

Compared to eternity, the NC time will be very brief. During the hour of the NC, the Holy City will become Jesus, the place of worship. File this very important data point away for later consideration because understanding the concept that the NC has been stated to be one hour long per the eternity clock will help unravel prophecy later.

Jesus knew the disciples were fishermen who were tasked to start the biggest worldwide enterprise that ever existed. He also knew that their work would be negatively impacted by false teachers. We have very limited documentation of what happened to the disciples during the start-up of the NC. After Jesus' sacrifice, the documentation for the startup of the NC is presented entirely through the book of Acts and some letters mostly attributed to Paul. The book of Acts is written by the same author who wrote Luke, who admittedly was not an eyewitness and doesn't name himself or his sources. The focus of Acts is on Peter, who is referenced seventy-two times and Paul, with over two hundred mentions. Andrew and James are ignored, and John is only mentioned several times when he is with Peter. In summary, the book of Acts and the letters do not represent Jesus' chosen eyewitnesses except for emphasizing Peter and a few short letters written by John, including the one just previously referenced.

Except for a few hidden gems like 1 John 2:18–19, the painted picture we have of the early church does not come from the testimony of Jesus' eyewitnesses; it is at best second-hand information provided by others. God is a God of evidence. Besides the three Gospels, we have no eyewitness testimony other than a few brief letters and the book of Revelation to describe the NC. This is not accidental. We have those few priceless words of John warning us not to believe the ECFs who followed the disciples, and this message will be repeated by God throughout prophecy.

If you are now anxiety-stricken over what I've written, be patient, and thank God for the prophecy he provided us, because through it, God provided a complete accounting of what happened to Jesus' evidence package. Like I stated earlier, the Billford vision let me know that prophecy is solid evidence of the future told in advance. Therefore, in our search for the evidence package for Jesus and to determine what happened to it, I rely heavily on the Olivet Discourse, Daniel and Revelation prophecy as facts, not predictions. The evidence obtained through analysis of them provides the true, complete future of the NC.

Leading to the analysis of prophecy, in summary, we have the following foundation for Jesus' evidence package:

1. Jesus spoke for God:

   > "He who doesn't love me doesn't keep my words. The word which you hear isn't mine, but the Father's who sent me." (John 14:24)

   > "I and the Father are one." (John 10:30)

2. Prophets who wrote the Messiah prophecy were the only people God gave authority to speak for him:

   > But the prophet who speaks a word presumptuously in my name, which I have not commanded him to speak, or who speaks in the name of other gods, that same prophet shall die." You may say in your heart, "How shall we know the word which Yahweh has not spoken?" When a prophet speaks in Yahweh's name, if the thing doesn't follow, nor happen, that is the thing which Yahweh has not spoken. The prophet has spoken it presumptuously. You shall not be afraid of him. (Deuteronomy 18:20–22)

3. Jesus validated that Moses spoke for God because Moses prophesied about Jesus:

   "For if you believed Moses, you would believe me; for he wrote about me." (John 5:46)

4. Jesus validated the OT prophets speaking for God because they also prophesied him as the Messiah:

   "Don't think that I came to destroy the law or the prophets. I didn't come to destroy, but to fulfill." (Matthew 5:17)

   "But all this has happened that the Scriptures of the prophets might be fulfilled." (Matthew 26:56)

5. But prophets only spoke for God if the Messiah is proven to have come in fulfilment of their prophecy. Testimony is required to prove Jesus as the Messiah:

   At the mouth of two witnesses, or three witnesses, he who is to die shall be put to death. At the mouth of one witness he shall not be put to death. (Deuteronomy 17:6)

   One witness shall not rise up against a man for any iniquity, or for any sin that he sins. At the mouth of two witnesses, or at the mouth of three witnesses, shall a matter be established. (Deuteronomy 19:15)

6. Jesus validated that the testimony requirements applied to him:

   "If I testify about myself, my witness is not valid." (John 5:31)

   "But the testimony which I receive is not from man. However, I say these things that you may be saved." (John 5:34)

   The Pharisees therefore said to him, "You testify about yourself. Your testimony is not valid." (John 8:13) "It's also written in your law that the testimony of two people is valid. I am one who testifies about myself, and the Father who sent me testifies about me." (John 8:17–18)

7. Jesus selected four disciples to be his eyewitnesses to document their testimony between 30 and 33 AD; they will document their testimony prior to their persecution and execution:

   > As he sat on the Mount of Olives opposite the temple, Peter, James, John, and Andrew asked him privately, (Mark 13:3)
   >
   > "But watch yourselves, for they will deliver you up to councils. You will be beaten in synagogues. You will stand before rulers and kings for my sake, for a testimony to them. The Good News must first be preached to all the nations. When they lead you away and deliver you up, don't be anxious beforehand or premeditate what you will say, but say whatever will be given you in that hour. For it is not you who speak, but the Holy Spirit. (Mark 13:9–11)

8. Jesus ensured that his eyewitnesses would provide the most accurate testimony ever documented because God was going to help them remember the details and write them down:

   > "I have said these things to you while still living with you. But the Counselor, the Holy Spirit, whom the Father will send in my name, will teach you all things, and will remind you of all that I said to you. (John 14:25–26)

9. Jesus took his selected eyewitnesses everywhere he went so that they would observe everything Jesus said and did, and their testimony would be complete:

   - The synagogue ruler's daughter raised back to life from the dead (Mark 5:36–43)
   - The transfiguration of Jesus when he appeared with Moses and Elijah, proves that there is eternal life. (Mark 9:2–4)
   - Jesus, through his Olivet Discourse, prophesied the future of those four disciples and assigned them to be his chosen eyewitnesses (Mark 13:1–37)
   - Jesus preparing for his execution (Mark 14:32–42)

10. Jesus promised that his words would not be affected by time nor translations:

    > Heaven and earth will pass away, but my words will not pass away. (Mark 13:31)

11. Jesus breathed the Holy Spirit into the disciples to get them started on documenting their testimony in 30 AD, the first evening of Jesus' resurrection:

> When he had said this, he breathed on them, and said to them, "Receive the Holy Spirit! (John 20:22)

12. The testimony of Jesus' eyewitnesses was completed on the day God's protection of the disciples ended, and false teachers began persecuting followers of Jesus; the start of the great tribulation:

> [59] They stoned Stephen as he called out, saying, "Lord Jesus, receive my spirit!" [60] He kneeled down and cried with a loud voice, "Lord, don't hold this sin against them!" [1] When he had said this, he fell asleep. Saul was consenting to his death. A great persecution arose against the assembly which was in Jerusalem in that day. (Acts 7:59—8:1)

After each major portion of this investigation, I will present a summary of the evidence supporting twelve specific, discrete periods of the time of Jesus. The first, from the previous chapters, follows:

THE FOUNDATION FOR JESUS EVIDENCE

1. Jesus is God born as a man with a mission to start the NC (6 BC)
   a. Deuteronomy 18:20–22—Prophets who prophesied the coming of Jesus spoke for God
   b. Matthew 5:17—The OT prophets prophesied Jesus and spoke for God (e.g., Isaiah 7:14, Micah 5:2, Zachariah 12:10, Hosea 11:1, Plasm 22:18 and Malachi 3:1, et al)
   c. Matthew 26:56—Jesus came to fulfil OT prophets' prophecy
   d. John 5:46—Moses prophesied about Jesus and spoke for God
2. Satan attempted to stop the NC from starting (6 BC)
3. Jesus' mission to teach, heal and perform miracles (26–30 AD)
   a. John 5:31, 34, 8:13, 17–18—Jesus affirmed that he must be proven through eyewitness testimony in accordance with Deuteronomy 17:6 and 19:15

b. John 10:24–25—God has testified on behalf of Jesus through his works

c. John 3:34, 8:58, 10:30, 12:49–50, 14:24—Jesus claimed to speak for God and stated he was God

d. John 14:25–26—Jesus promised his eyewitnesses that he would provide them with help to remember everything Jesus said and did and to explain all the details

e. Mark 13:5–6—Jesus warned his disciples that they would be led astray and train false teachers who would then lead many people astray with their teaching

f. Mark 13:3, 10—Jesus selected four disciples, James, John, Peter, and Andrew, to be his eyewitnesses to document their testimony for all people of the world

g. Mark 5:36–43, 9:2–4, 13:1–37, 14:32–42—Jesus took his eyewitnesses with him privately to observe all the details of his life, to ensure their testimony is complete

4. Jesus' sacrifice and resurrection (30 AD)

    a. John 20:21–22—Jesus delivered the promised Holy Spirit on resurrection day to help his eyewitnesses get their testimony exact

5. Second half of Jesus' seven-year mission (30–33 AD)

    a. Mark 13:10—assignment given to James, John, Peter, and Andrew to provide their testimony

    b. Mark 13:31—The words of Jesus will remain unchanged throughout all time

6. Start of the NC, Great Tribulation, and the Testimonies are completed (33 AD)

    a. Mark 13:9, 11—persecution of the disciples starts

7. Generation of the Disciples (33–67 AD)

    a. 1 John 2:18–19—Those the disciples chose to succeed them were false teachers—antichrists, who were taking over the NC

8. The NC (33—2333 AD)

   a. Deuteronomy 17:6, 19:15—Once Jesus' mission is completed, two- or three-witnesses are required per the Law of God to prove him to all future nations and people
   b. Mark 13:31—Jesus promised to forever protect his words from corruption
   c. John 2:4, 4:21—Jesus referred to the NC as being an hour long, but this is per the eternal time clock
9. First half of the NC—the reign of the Beast (33—1333 AD)
   a. Acts 8:1—The great tribulation started with the stoning death of Stephen
10. Second half of Jesus' NC—Jesus' 1000-year reign with his chosen ones (1333–2333 AD)
11. The Time of the End (2333-?)
12. Judgement

Next is the analysis and discussion of prophecy that will support Jesus' evidence package and provide the evidence that reveals what happened to the package Jesus left the world.

8

Olivet Discourse Prophecy

The first section of prophecy to be reviewed is the Olivet Discourse because it provided the foundation for Jesus' evidence package. The following analysis will provide additional proof that the Matthew version is copied from Mark. The details in it further support Jesus' evidence package rather than end-time ART theology as claimed by the CRLs through their theology. Separated into distinct actions to allow analysis:

1. A DISCIPLE POINTS OUT THE SPLENDOR OF THE TEMPLE BUILDINGS

> Matthew 24:1
> Jesus went out from the temple, and was going on his way. His disciples came to him to show him the buildings of the temple.
>
> Mark 13:1
> As he went forth out of the temple, one of his disciples said to him, "Teacher, see what kind of stones and what kind of buildings!"

Analysis: Mark's author was present because he pointed out that ONE disciple brought up the "kind of stones" and "kind of buildings," whereas in Matthew, it is a generic comment that "His disciples came to him to show him the buildings of the temple." The account in Mark provides specific details, but the account in Matthew is a copy that has left off these details to make it a general description. It's been reworded a bit to make it seem like Matthew, a disciple of Jesus, is providing his eyewitness testimony of the same event described by Mark's author.

2. JESUS RESPONDS

Matthew 24:2
But he answered them, "You see all of these things, don't you? Most certainly I tell you, there will not be left here one stone on another, that will not be thrown down."

Mark 13:2
Jesus said to him, "Do you see these great buildings? There will not be left here one stone on another, which will not be thrown down."

Analysis: Mark's author claimed Jesus stated, "Do you see these great buildings?", which follows the logic of the first verse. In Matthew, the scope of the discussion is expanded to "You see all of these things don't you?" The two versions would be nearly carbon copies, it were not for that one strategic change. The copied and edited version in Matthew has been expanded to widen the scope of the discussion to "ALL THESE THINGS," and with the additional comment and minor rewording, those who edited it again want you to believe that the author was Matthew, who was present to hear those words.

3. THE DISCIPLES ASK FOR MORE DETAILS:

Matthew 24:3
As he sat on the Mount of Olives, the disciples came to him privately, saying, "Tell us, when will these things be? What is the sign of your coming, and of the end of the age?"

Mark 13:3–4
[3] As he sat on the Mount of Olives opposite the temple, Peter, James, John, and Andrew asked him privately, [4] "Tell us, when will these things be? What is the sign that these things are all about to be fulfilled?"

Analysis: Mark's author tells us the location "opposite the temple" and who was present "Peter, James, John, and Andrew, who "asked him privately." There are no situational eyewitness details in Matthew that have been added to indicate it is anything but a copy. Therefore, the account in Matthew is again copied and changed just a bit. Mark's author recorded, "What is the sign that these things are all about to be fulfilled?" The copy in Matthew has the disciple's question edited to expand it to ask, "What is the sign of your coming, AND OF THE END OF THE AGE?" This second strategic change to Matthew has changed the message of Mark from a private discussion with four disciples about the destruction of the temple, to a discussion with all the disciples about the end time. Now you know why CRLs always refer to the version in Matthew to explain the Olivet Discourse. The message in Mark is about the future of the disciples and the NC, but the message in the copied and edited version in Matthew supports ART theology.

The false teachers removed the names of the four disciples and replaced them with the generic term "the disciples," but they revealed their deceit by claiming "the disciples came to him PRIVATELY." Jesus was with his disciples and would only go privately with four of them, not the whole group.

4. A WARNING FROM JESUS TO BEWARE OF FALSE TEACHERS.

> Matthew 24:4–5
> [4] Jesus answered them, "Be careful that no one leads you astray. [5] For many will come in my name, saying, 'I am the Christ,' and will lead many astray.
>
> Mark 13:5–6
> [5] Jesus, answering, began to tell them, "Be careful that no one leads you astray. [6] For many will come in my name, saying, 'I am he!' and will lead many astray."

Analysis: Matthew is an exact duplicate again, with some word manipulation to make it appear as though the author of Matthew is a disciple of Jesus who was also present to hear this exchange. Since Matthew was edited to have ALL the disciples possible, this made it possible.

Jesus was asked when the temple would also be destroyed (Mark 13:2), but this answer wasn't about the buildings. Yes, the temple buildings will be destroyed, but Jesus addressed how he will replace the temple, then afterwards false teachers will lead the disciples astray. Then the false teachers who lead the disciples astray will claim they are Jesus, and they will lead many people astray.

5. JESUS WARNS OF MISLEADING TOPICS

> Matthew 24:6–8
> [6] You will hear of wars and rumors of wars. See that you aren't troubled, for all this must happen, but the end is not yet. [7] For

nation will rise against nation, and kingdom against kingdom; and there will be famines, plagues, and earthquakes in various places. [8] But all these things are the beginning of birth pains.

Mark 13:7–8
[7] "When you hear of wars and rumors of wars, don't be troubled. For those must happen, but the end is not yet. [8] For nation will rise against nation, and kingdom against kingdom. There will be earthquakes in various places. There will be famines and troubles. These things are the beginning of birth pains.

Analysis: These accounts are again near exact duplicates, with words rearranged in Matthew to make it appear as though Matthew was an eyewitness who was present but recorded the words of Jesus slightly differently. Jesus has warned four of his disciples that they will experience natural disasters, wars, and hear rumors of wars. But Jesus told the four that what they will witness "are the beginning of birth pains," so they are not to worry about these things because "the end is not yet." Jesus boldly told you that this discussion has nothing to do with the end time.

6. JESUS ASSIGNS FOUR DISCIPLES TO BE EYEWITNESSES

Matthew 24:9–14
[9] "Then they will deliver you up to oppression and will kill you. You will be hated by all of the nations for my name's sake. [10] Then many will stumble, and will deliver up one another, and will hate one another. [11] Many false prophets will arise and will lead many astray. [12] Because iniquity will be multiplied, the love of many will grow cold. [13] But he who endures to the end will be saved. [14] This Good News of the Kingdom will be preached in the whole world for a testimony to all the nations, and then the end will come.

Mark 13:9–13
[9] "But watch yourselves, for they will deliver you up to councils. You will be beaten in synagogues. You will stand before rulers and kings for my sake, for a testimony to them. [10] The Good News must first be preached to all the nations. [11] When they lead you away and deliver you up, don't be anxious beforehand or premeditate what you will say, but say whatever will be given you in that hour. For it is not you who speak, but the Holy Spirit. [12] "Brother will deliver

up brother to death, and the father his child. Children will rise up against parents and cause them to be put to death. [13] You will be hated by all men for my name's sake, but he who endures to the end will be saved.

Analysis: These two versions have the same details, but in Matthew, that copy has been manipulated to point to the end time. In Matthew, the disciples will be "delivered up and killed." After the disciples are killed, "many will stumble", then "false teachers will arise." Then the magic words pinpointing the end of time are presented: "he who endures to the end will be saved." Finally, the Good News of Jesus will spread around the world to all nations, "then the end will come." If Matthew wasn't a copy from Mark, I would almost believe the Olivet Discourse to be about the end time that occurs once the Good News of Jesus reaches the whole world.

But then we already went through the analysis of the original in Mark to find that Jesus provided the future for those four eyewitnesses and appointed them to provide their testimony. Matthew is a phony edited version to have you believing that the ECFs were holy men of God, but watch out because at the end time, the boogeyman antichrist will appear to lead many astray. Jesus, through Mark's author told you he was going to ensure that you had evidence to find the truth. John, through his letter 1 John 2:18–19, told you to believe his words and the words of Jesus, but reject what you are being told by the ECFs and those who follow them.

7. JESUS REFERS TO THE ABOMINATION OF DESOLATION

Matthew 24:15–16
[15] "When, therefore, you see the abomination of desolation, which was spoken of through Daniel the prophet, standing in the holy place (let the reader understand), [16] then let those who are in Judea flee to the mountains.

Mark 13:14
[14] "But when you see the abomination of desolation, spoken of by Daniel the prophet, standing where it ought not" (let the reader understand), "then let those who are in Judea flee to the mountains,

Analysis: The version in Matthew is again nearly an exact duplicate of what is presented in Mark, with a few minor word changes and rearrangement. In

Matthew, the Abomination of Desolation (AOD) follows the comment about the end time. This connection is used to claim that Daniel's reference to the AOD addresses the end time. In the Mark version, Jesus has told James, John, Peter, and Andrew that they will see the AOD. Since Acts 12:2 documents James being executed by Herod, he is dead sometime near 40 AD. According to this correlation, the AOD "spoken of by Daniel" MUST happen prior to that year. You will see later how prophecy explains that the AOD starts the day the great tribulation begins with the stoning death of Stephen in 33 AD (Acts 8:1), which is the same time the eyewitnesses of Jesus finished their testimonies.

8. THE START OF THE GREAT PERSECUTION:

> Matthew 24:17–22
> [17] Let him who is on the housetop not go down to take out the
> things that are in his house. [18] Let him who is in the field not re-
> turn back to get his clothes. [19] But woe to those who are with child
> and to nursing mothers in those days! [20] Pray that your flight will
> not be in the winter nor on a Sabbath, [21] for then there will be
> great suffering, such as has not been from the beginning of the
> world until now, no, nor ever will be. [22] Unless those days had been
> shortened, no flesh would have been saved. But for the sake of the
> chosen ones, those days will be shortened.

> Mark 13:15–20
> [15] and let him who is on the housetop not go down, nor enter in,
> to take anything out of his house. [16] Let him who is in the field
> not return back to take his cloak. [17] But woe to those who are with
> child and to those who nurse babies in those days! [18] Pray that
> your flight won't be in the winter. [19] For in those days there will be
> oppression, such as there has not been the like from the beginning
> of the creation which God created until now, and never will be. [20]
> Unless the Lord had shortened the days, no flesh would have been
> saved; but for the sake of the chosen ones, whom he picked out, he
> shortened the days.

Analysis: The Matthew version is nearly a carbon copy of what is written in Mark, but with a few insignificant editorial changes to make it look like the author is present to hear the discussion. When the false teachers take control of the NC, they will persecute and even execute anyone who doesn't agree with their ownership. But the Lord "shortened the days" so false teachers will at one point lose their authority over the people of God during the NC.

9. JESUS AGAIN WARNS ABOUT FALSE TEACHERS

> Matthew 24:23–29
> [23] "Then if any man tells you, 'Behold, here is the Christ!' or,
> 'There!' don't believe it. [24] For false christs and false prophets will
> arise, and they will show great signs and wonders, so as to lead
> astray, if possible, even the chosen ones. [25] "Behold, I have told
> you beforehand. [26] "If therefore they tell you, 'Behold, he is in the
> wilderness,' don't go out; or 'Behold, he is in the inner rooms,' don't
> believe it. [27] For as the lightning flashes from the east, and is seen
> even to the west, so will the coming of the Son of Man be. [28] For
> wherever the carcass is, that is where the vultures gather together.
> [29] "But immediately after the suffering of those days, the sun will
> be darkened, the moon will not give its light, the stars will fall from
> the sky, and the powers of the heavens will be shaken;

> Mark 13:21–25
> [21] Then if anyone tells you, 'Look, here is the Christ!' or, 'Look,
> there!' don't believe it. [22] For false christs and false prophets will
> arise and will show signs and wonders, that they may lead astray,
> if possible, even the chosen ones. [23] But you watch. "Behold, I have
> told you all things beforehand. [24] But in those days, after that op-
> pression, the sun will be darkened, the moon will not give its light,
> [25] the stars will be falling from the sky, and the powers that are in
> the heavens will be shaken.

Analysis: The version in Matthew is again nearly an exact duplicate of what is presented in Mark, but with a few very important changes. In Mark, Jesus says, "But you watch", which is another direct warning to these four disciples that they will be impacted and overwhelmed by the actions of false teachers. That key phrase has purposely been edited out of Matthew. The phrase "so will be the coming of the Son of Man" has been added to the copied version in Matthew to again support the Olivet Discourse end-time ART theology with a second coming of Jesus. We learn here that the false teachers will be removing the light of the world.

10. THE GREAT PERSECUTION WILL END

Matthew 24:30–31
30 and then the sign of the Son of Man will appear in the sky. Then
all the tribes of the earth will mourn, and they will see the Son of
Man coming on the clouds of the sky with power and great glory.
31 He will send out his angels with a great sound of a trumpet,
and they will gather together his chosen ones from the four winds,
from one end of the sky to the other.

Mark 13:26–27
26 Then they will see the Son of Man coming in clouds with great
power and glory. 27 Then he will send out his angels, and will gather
together his chosen ones from the four winds, from the ends of the
earth to the ends of the sky.

Analysis: As discussed earlier, the Matthew version has been edited to provide a visible physical appearance of Jesus. The claim that "the Son of Man will appear in the sky" is not found in the original. These four disciples are told, "then THEY will see the Son of Man COMING IN CLOUDS." Jesus has not said "YOU will see the Son of Man," he said "THEY WILL", meaning that this event will happen AFTER the time of the disciples. This event will come after the disciples have died, and as discussed earlier, since Jesus is IN CLOUDS, it signifies a spiritual change to the NC. The "chosen ones" will be explained later through prophecy as the martyrs who will be killed by the false teachers during the first half of the NC. The false teachers who John stated were taking control of the NC will reign, but they have a decreed ending when Jesus returns to the NC to reign—but it won't be a visible physical reign.

11. JESUS IS THE TREE OF LIFE

Matthew 24:32–33
32 "Now from the fig tree learn her parable. When its branch has
now become tender, and puts forth its leaves, you know that the
summer is near. 33 Even so you also, when you see all these things,
know that it is near, even at the doors."

Mark 13:28–29
28 "Now from the fig tree, learn this parable. When the branch has
now become tender and produces its leaves, you know that the

summer is near; [29] even so you also, when you see these things coming to pass, know that it is near, at the doors.

Analysis: Again, a near carbon copy is presented in Matthew, taken from the Gospel of Mark. The disciples were commissioned to share the Good News of Jesus. Remember the fig tree that didn't bear fruit, so Jesus destroyed it (Mark 11:12–21)? Like the fig tree with green leaves, the eyewitnesses will document their testimony to start the NC, and there is hope that the Good News of Jesus will spread throughout the world. But the fruit of the tree will be impacted by false teachers, so Jesus has promised to deal with them. Like the fig tree, Jesus will destroy those who corrupt the NC.

12. THE DISCIPLES WILL WITNESS EVERYTHING

Matthew 24:34–35
[34] "Most certainly I tell you, this generation will not pass away until all these things are accomplished. [35] Heaven and earth will pass away, but my words will not pass away."

Mark 13:30–31
[30] Most certainly I say to you, this generation will not pass away until all these things happen. [31] Heaven and earth will pass away, but my words will not pass away.

Analysis: Again, a near exact duplicate is presented in Matthew that has been copied from Mark. It's obvious that every experience Jesus told them "you will. . ." is going to be experienced by the disciples. The generation of the disciples will experience every prophecy that Jesus prophesied in the Olivet Discourse, except for one prophecy of the change coming to the NC later when Jesus spiritually returns. The Matthew interpretations claim the Olivet Discourse is all about ART Jesus' second coming theology.

OLIVET DISCOURSE JESUS EVIDENCE

1. Jesus is God born as a man with a mission to start the NC (6 BC)
2. Satan attempted to stop the NC from starting (6 BC)
3. Jesus' mission to teach, heal and perform miracles (26–30 AD)
4. Jesus' sacrifice and resurrection (30 AD)

5. Second half of Jesus' seven-year mission (30–33 AD)
6. Start of the NC, the Great Tribulation, and the AOD (33 AD)
   a. Mark 13:14—Jesus' chosen eyewitnesses will observe the AOD as the false teachers replace the temple of Jesus with their brand of religion
7. Generation of the Disciples (33–67 AD)
   a. Mark 13:9, 11—Jesus foretold the persecution and executions of his four inner circle disciples John, Andrew, Peter, and James
8. The NC (33–2333 AD)
   a. Matthew 24:1–35—False teachers edited the copied version of the Olivet Discourse in Matthew to support ART theology and hide the beast in the time of the end
9. First half of the NC—the reign of the Beast (33–1333 AD)
   a. Mark 13:15–20—Jesus foretold the great tribulation also called the great persecution
   b. Mark 13:21–25—False teachers who Jesus referred to as the beast will remove the light of the world and persecute anyone who doesn't submit to their reign
10. Second half of Jesus' NC—Jesus' 1000-year reign with his chosen ones (1333–2333 AD)
    a. Mark 13:26–27—Jesus foretold the end of the great tribulation with a spiritual return in the clouds to free the Gospel from the grips of the beast
11. The Time of the End (2333-?)
12. Judgement

9

Revelation: NC Part 1

A SUMMARY OF THE NC presented in Revelation 6:1—11:19 begins with the seven seals. The first seal describes Jesus coming to the world (Revelation 6:1–2), followed by a second seal that describes Satan, who came to destroy the NC (Revelation 6:3–4). Matthew's author provided a great summary of Satan's actions through King Herod's attempts to eliminate the NC before it even started (Matthew 2:1–18). But God protected Jesus when he was a child from harm (Matthew 2:19–20).

The third seal describes Satan and false teachers in charge of the NC. During their reign, people are starving for the word of God because followers of Jesus are only getting fed portions of the bread of life and the living water of Jesus (Revelation 6:5–6). The fourth seal describes the ruthlessness of the false teachers as they persecute and kill those who reject their claim of owning the NC. The pale horse in that fourth seal symbolizes the word of God that started out as the words of Jesus but then became a mix of Satan's and Jesus' words (Revelation 6:7–8). The fifth seal describes false teachers using force to control the NC as they execute people who reject their claim to be speaking for God (Revelation 6:9–11). As time goes on, the power of the false teachers grows and spreads, and with it, the numbers of those executed for staying loyal to Jesus add up. The sixth seal reveals that false teachers working with Satan completely removed Jesus, the light of the world, from the NC (Revelation 6:12–17).

When the number of those executed reaches a decreed number of 144000, a change will come to the NC (Revelation 7:1–13). The reign of the false teachers has come to an end, and with it, the great tribulation also ends:

> He said to me, "These are those who came out of the great suffering. They washed their robes and made them white in the Lamb's blood. (Revelation 7:14)

The great tribulation started with the stoning death of Stephen in 33 AD and ended when the 144,000th decreed martyr was killed for rejecting the false teacher message that came from Satan. Even though Jesus had been eliminated from the NC, a multitude of people suffered through the persecution to follow the word of God to be cleansed of their sin and ended up at the throne with God (Revelation 7:14–17).

Then, at the end of the great tribulation, the reign of Satan and the false teachers ends with a prophesied big change to the NC:

> When he opened the seventh seal, there was silence in heaven for about half an hour. (Revelation 8:1)

There are two important aspects to this last seal. First, we are told that heaven will go silent and second, we are told that heaven will be silent for "about half an hour." Recall the analysis earlier proving that the NC is an hour long in eternity time (1 John 2:18). An hour isn't a long time on earth, but it is a long time when comparing time on earth to the time clock of eternity. Once you physically die, you will end up in your eternal destination, where an hour of eternity will be like hundreds and even thousands of years on earth. Choose your path wisely, because at your physical death, your fate will be sealed, and with it, your final destination will be set for eternity.

With the NC lasting for an hour, the seventh seal tells us that there will be two nearly equal NC periods of time. The first half of the NC was the great tribulation with false teachers reigning over the NC through force, persecution, and executions. The second half of the NC will be a time when heaven is silent. Heaven is a place of worship of Jesus; therefore, if heaven is silent, Jesus must have left. Prophecy explains a time when Jesus leaves heaven:

> I saw thrones, and they sat on them, and judgment was given to them. I saw the souls of those who had been beheaded for the testimony of Jesus and for the word of God, and such as didn't worship the beast nor his image, and didn't receive the mark on their forehead and on their hand. They lived and reigned with Christ for a thousand years. (Revelation 20:4)

This section of Revelation describes the 144,000 who were executed for rejecting the false teachers. The false teachers who are followers of Satan are referred to here as the "beast." Those executed during the great tribulation, the first half of the NC, are resurrected to reign and live with "Christ for a thousand years."

Jesus confirmed that the return of Jesus will be "in clouds" as he sends out his angels to gather the 144,000 "chosen ones" (Mark 13:26–27). Halfway through the NC, Jesus returned to reign with the resurrected martyrs who were executed during the great tribulation. This is not a visible physical return of Jesus; it represents a spiritual freedom from the reign of the beast.

Revelation describes another time when Jesus will return, and it will be a visible appearance:

> Behold, he is coming with the clouds, and every eye will see him, including those who pierced him. All the tribes of the earth will mourn over him. Even so, Amen. (Revelation 1:7)

In this summary, "every eye will see him," so Jesus will be visible. But the appearance described in this verse is not a welcome appearance because those "who pierced him" and "all the tribes of the earth"—the people who have rejected Jesus, "will mourn." This group of people is not happy to witness Jesus because it is the time of judgment and punishment for their rejection of Jesus.

The first half of the NC was described through the prophecy of the seals. The second half of the NC, the thousand-year reign of Jesus with the 144,000 martyrs (Revelation 7:1–13), is described through Revelation 8:2—11:15. The first thing Jesus tells us about the second half of the NC is that it will also be a time of trouble because God rejects the prayers going up to heaven (Revelation 8:3–5). Seven trumpet blasts will explain why the prayers are rejected (Revelation 8:6). The first trumpet is a message that describes the popular fire and brimstone CRL message that focuses on punishment rather than eternal life through Jesus (Revelation 8:7). The second trumpet describes the impact of following the words of others besides Jesus that are being taught by CRLs (Revelation 8:8–9). The third trumpet describes the created theology that has permeated throughout the word of God to mislead followers of Jesus (Revelation 8:10–11). It is referred to as Wormwood—an infestation of damaging words that have infiltrated the word of God. The fourth trumpet is about carefully crafted cherry-picked messages that will mislead many (Revelation 8:12). All four trumpet blasts result in death, destruction, and times of trouble for those searching for the word of God through Jesus.

There is a warning about three "woes" that will come through the last three trumpets (Revelation 8:13). The fifth trumpet signifies the pit of the abyss being opened. Flipping through prophecy, we find the description of the abyss pit:

> I saw an angel coming down out of heaven, having the key of the abyss and a great chain in his hand. [2] He seized the dragon, the old serpent, who is the devil and Satan, who deceives the whole inhabited earth, and bound him for a thousand years, [3] and cast him into the abyss, and shut it and sealed it over him, that he should deceive the nations no more until the thousand years were finished. After this, he must be freed for a short time. (Revelation 20:1–3)

For a thousand years, Satan has been locked up during the reign of Jesus, but after the thousand years, Satan will be freed "for a short time." The second half of the NC has ended—the thousand-year reign of Jesus ends when Satan is freed for his short time

Satan is released from the pit of the abyss, and for five months the wrath of God will be poured out (Revelation 9:1–11) on those who have rejected him:

> In those days people will seek death, and will in no way find it. They will desire to die, and death will flee from them. (Revelation 9:6)

The first portion of the "short time" for Satan to deceive the people of the world is described through the fifth trumpet as a period of war, sickness, and destitution so terrible that people will want to die, but God will keep them alive. This five-month period has described the first of the three woes (Revelation 9:12), and there are two more to come.

The sixth trumpet describes an army of Satan numbering 200 million, and during this end time, there will be plagues, hazardous gases, war, and overall devastation for the people of the world, but none of them will turn to God (Revelation 9:13–21). The end time is also described through the following:

> [7] When the thousand years are over, Satan will be released from his prison [8] and will go out to deceive the nations in the four corners of the earth—Gog and Magog—and to gather them for battle. In number they are like the sand on the seashore. [9] They went up over the width of the earth and surrounded the camp of the saints and the beloved city. Fire came down out of heaven from God and devoured them. (Revelation 20:7–9)

Notice that at the time of the end, there is a "camp" of saints, so there are only a few followers of Jesus remaining in the whole world. On the flip side, the followers of Satan number "like the sand on the seashore," he has gathered them for war. Consider what you have heard about ART theology with a rapture of followers of Jesus—there is no rapture because there are only a few followers of Jesus remaining in the world. No timeline is given for how long the final battles with Satan will last. However, the next description from Revelation is complete destruction, because "Fire came down out of heaven from God and devoured them."

Prior to the seventh trumpet, there is an unusual twist to the chronological account, as an angel is described coming down from the sky with a little book (Revelation 10:1–6). Only Jesus can read the little book, and John was told to taste it because "It will make your stomach bitter, but in your mouth it will be as sweet as honey." Revelation presents a set of books that has Jesus judging people based on their actions, but this is one book rather than a set—it is the book of life. Those with their name in the book of life have found salvation through Jesus, but those whose names aren't in the book find God's contempt.

John followed the instructions and tasted the book to find it sweet because his name was in there, but it made him sick because of all the people who weren't saved and faced death and Hades in the lake of fire (Revelation 10:8–10 and 20:12–15). As the discussion of the little book ends, there is the following key message:

> They told me, "You must prophesy again over many peoples, nations, languages, and kings." (Revelation 10:11)

What is presented next is prophecy for ALL people. And what is the message? Two of Jesus' eyewitnesses provided a symbolic sacrifice, welcoming all the people of the world into the NC (Revelation 11:1–13).

Two of Jesus' eyewitnesses were prophesied to provide their testimony, and when they finish, they will be executed. These two eyewitnesses are represented as the olive tree branch (Revelation 11:4) that extended the sacrifice of Jesus to the Gentiles to welcome them into the NC. The two witnesses performed miracles with a mission that, as you will see later through analysis of Daniel and Revelation prophecy, was the exact length of time of Jesus' 1260-day mission for teaching, healing and performing miracles. Just like Jesus, they were sacrificed and then raised from the dead. Jesus came as the promised Messiah as the sacrifice for the Jews. The two witnesses represented Jesus' sacrifice to the Gentiles.

Jesus selected four witnesses, James, John, Peter, and Andrew, to provide their testimony. In the Bible, there are two letters attributed to Peter, but both have similarities to letters written by Paul. Therefore, Peter, as the author of those letters, is questionable. Furthermore, 1 Peter states that a scribe wrote the letter for Peter (1 Peter 5:2), indicating that if that letter is from Peter, he couldn't write. If Peter couldn't write, then Andrew, like his brother living in the same house, couldn't write either. Why would Jesus, who knows all, select Peter and Andrew to be eyewitnesses to testify on his behalf for ALL future people, when he knows they can't write? The simple answer is that Jesus had another job for them as the two witnesses (Revelation 11:1–13).

Peter and Andrew weren't decreed to be like James and John, who would document their testimony of Jesus for ALL future people of the world. John documented the eyewitness testimony of Peter and Andrew, who sacrificed themselves like Jesus to extend God's invitation of salvation through Jesus to ALL the people of the world. The testimony of Andrew and Peter may not have been written with their own hand, but we have an amazing record of their testimony and sacrifice documented by John in Revelation.

We also have history backing up the story of their testimony. The fire that engulfed Rome in 64 AD has always been a mystery—that is, until now:

> If anyone desires to harm them, fire proceeds out of their mouth and devours their enemies. If anyone desires to harm them, he must be killed in this way. (Revelation 11:5)

Who were the enemies of the two witnesses? Those who were aligned with Satan—the religious leaders who led the coup to take control of the NC with assistance from their coconspirators, the Roman government officials. Fire destroyed Rome in 64 AD. Therefore, we know that Peter and Andrew were in Rome during that fire because they burned it down. After they finished their 1,260-day testimony, the two witnesses were executed in Jerusalem just as Jesus was (Revelation 11:7). We also know that false teachers "trample on the holy city for 42 months" (Revelation 11:2). Therefore, putting that information together we can determine that after the two witnesses burned down Rome with fire from heaven, they were transported to Jerusalem where they testified for 1,260 days, the 42 months that the beast trampled on the holy city. This summary dates their execution and resurrection to 67 AD.

The two witnesses, like Jesus, rose from the dead and then ascended into heaven. Note that James is also recorded as being executed prior to the two witnesses (Acts 12:2). With Jesus telling his four witnesses they will all face death (Mark 13:9), we don't have a record of it, but we can be assured that John was also executed.

Peter and Andrew were the chosen witnesses to provide their testimony that welcomed ALL people into the Kingdom of God. God welcomes you, me, and everyone else who lives during the NC into the eternal Kingdom of God. But the testimony of the two witnesses was rejected by most people at the time of their execution and resurrection, and it is still rejected by most people today. A person who rejects the testimony of the two witnesses has rejected God's invitation and will experience the second woe:

> The second woe is past. Behold, the third woe comes quickly. (Revelation 11:14)

Rejecting the invitation of Jesus and the two witnesses is the second woe because Jesus stated it would be:

> He who believes in him is not judged. He who doesn't believe has been judged already, because he has not believed in the name of the only born Son of God. (John 3:18)

Although the third woe isn't specifically defined, it's obvious that should you reject Jesus and the two witnesses, you have been judged, AND this means you have immediately been condemned to death and Hades. Reject Jesus and you have been judged, and the third woe—judgement and the fires of hell, will come to you quickly.

The end has also come for this account of the NC presented in the firsthalf of Revelation. After the time of the end with the wrath of God poured out, the seventh trumpet announces the arrival of the eternal kingdom of Jesus (Revelation 11:15). As the eternal kingdom is ushered in, the earth and everything in it is destroyed:

> God's temple that is in heaven was opened, and the ark of the Lord's covenant was seen in his temple. Lightnings, sounds, thunders, an earthquake, and great hail followed. (Revelation 11:19)

The great hail that follows is like the ending described in Revelation 16:21, the people of Satan will destroy the world.

REVELATION PROPHECY JESUS EVIDENCE

1. Jesus is God born as a man with a mission to start the NC (6 BC)
    a. Revelation 6:1–2—The first seal, Jesus comes to the world
2. Satan attempted to stop the NC from starting (6 BC)
    a. Revelation 6:3–4—The second seal, Satan comes to the world to stop Jesus
    b. Matthew 2:1–20—Satan attacked Jesus as a child, but God protected Jesus
3. Jesus' mission to teach, heal and perform miracles (26–30 AD)
4. Jesus' sacrifice and resurrection (30 AD)
5. Second half of Jesus' seven-year mission (30–33 AD)
6. Start of the NC, Great Tribulation, and the Testimonies are completed (33 AD)
7. Generation of the Disciples (33–67 AD)
    a. Acts 12:2—James is executed for Jesus
    b. Revelation 11:1–12—The mission of the two witnesses is to welcome the Gentiles into the NC
    c. Revelation 11:2—False teachers and Satan trample on the Holy City for 42 months
    d. Revelation 11:3–5—Peter and Andrew burn Rome and are transferred to Jerusalem, where they prophecy for 1,260 days—the same number of days as Jesus' mission
    e. Revelation 11:7–8—Andrew and Peter, as the two witnesses, are executed
8. The NC (33—2333 AD)
    a. 1 John 2:18—John confirmed that the NC is an hour long per eternity time
9. First half of the NC—the reign of the Beast (33—1333 AD)
    a. Revelation 6:5–6—The third seal describes the bread of life and the living water of Jesus provided by those in charge of the NC being in short supply

   b. Revelation 6:7–8—The fourth seal, the false teachers persecute and execute those who reject their message from Satan, with a bit of Jesus' words mixed in
   c. Revelation 6:9–10—The fifth seal tells of the ruthless leaders starting to execute those who reject their message
   d. Revelation 6:12–17—The sixth seal reveals that false teachers working with Satan have completely removed Jesus, the light of the world, from the NC
   e. Revelation 7:1–17—The decreed number of martyrs, 144000, has been executed as the false teacher's reign of terror, referred to as the great tribulation, ends

10. Second half of Jesus' NC—Jesus' 1000-year reign with his chosen ones (1333–2333 AD)
   a. Revelation 8:1—The seventh seal denotes the second half hour of the NC, starting as heaven goes silent because Jesus makes his spiritual return to the NC
   b. Revelation 20:4–5—There is a transition in the NC with the return of Jesus, who will reign with the 144000 martyrs for 1000 years
   c. Revelation 8:3–6—The prayers of people during the 1000-year reign of Jesus are rejected, indicating a time of trouble, and seven trumpet blasts will explain why
   d. Revelation 8:7—The first trumpet is a message of fire and brimstone that has CRLs focused on punishment rather than eternal life through Jesus
   e. Revelation 8:8–9—God meets with his people on a mountain, but the second trumpet describes something like a mountain—CRLs are pretending to be Jesus
   f. Revelation 8:10–11—Like wood-destroying pests and bitter water, the living water and word of God through Jesus, described in the third trumpet, is infested with theology and words of men
   g. Revelation 8:12—The fourth trumpet is about carefully crafted, cherry-picked messages of CRLs who ignore Jesus to mislead people through their message

11. The Time of the End (2333-?)
    a. Revelation 1:7—The tribes of the earth who have rejected Jesus will witness him coming in the clouds, and because of their punishment, they will mourn
    b. Revelation 8:13—The last three trumpets will highlight three woes that will befall those who have rejected Jesus
    c. Revelation 20:1–3—Satan is set free for a short while after his 1000 years in the pit of the Abyss during Jesus' reign is over
    d. Revelation 9:1–11—The wrath of God is poured out on those following Satan; the agony of this fifth trumpet is so bad that they will seek death, but God won't allow it
    e. Revelation 9:12—The five months of the fifth trumpet are the passing of the first woe
    f. Revelation 9:13–21—Plagues, war, and the fire of God are poured out during this undefined time when the wrath of God is poured out on the inhabitants of the earth
    g. Revelation 20:7–9—Satan, with his 200 million-strong army, controls the world and attacks the few remaining followers of Jesus who are in a camp
12. Judgement
    a. John 3:18—Believe in Jesus and you are not judged, reject and you have been judged
    b. Revelation 10:1—11:13—The second woe is for those who have rejected the testimony of Jesus and the two witnesses because they are immediately condemned
    c. Revelation 11:14—The third woe is the judgment and condemnation of those who have rejected Jesus that comes quickly after the second woe

You can see how the evidence package for Jesus is being supported through prophecy, with ample data points added to what has been provided in the Olivet Discourse. Next, I turn to the book of Daniel before finishing with the second half of Revelation. I think you'll find it fascinating to see how every vision described in the book of Daniel adds to the evidence package for Jesus.

10

Daniel's Prophecy and the New Covenant

DANIEL WAS BORN ABOUT 600 years before Jesus; therefore, although most of his visions describe the NC, there are some details of the OC in them too. There are six visions in Daniel that are analyzed in the order they are presented in Daniel's book:

1. NEBUCHADNEZZAR'S VISION OF THE STATUE (DANIEL 2:32–35)

The statue describes the rulers of the people of God from the days of Daniel to the time of the end. The following five Kingdoms are presented:

1. The Gold Kingdom: The Israelites, the people of God, have lost their kingdom and have been taken captive by the Babylonians, first to be ruled by their King Nebuchadnezzar. Nebuchadnezzar is initially a pagan, but through the influence of Daniel and visions from God, he became the gold standard of Godly rulers (Daniel 2:32). The Gold Kingdom lasted until Nebuchadnezzar's death in approximately 562 BC.
2. The Silver Kingdom: Silver is not as valuable as gold; therefore, this next period of rule over the Israelites will be inferior when compared to Nebuchadnezzar's reign (Daniel 2:32). After Nebuchadnezzar's Gold Kingdom, some rulers of the Israelites will be Godly, but others will follow evil. The Silver Kingdom went from 562 BC to 33 AD, the start of the NC.

3. The Bronze Kingdom: Bronze rulers over the people of God, who are now the people of nations, are neither gold nor silver. The Bronze rulers started replacing Jesus at the beginning of the NC by claiming to speak for God. They may appear like gold, but they are a cheap replacement (Daniel 2:32). ALL rulers during the Bronze Kingdom that lasted the first half of the NC from 33—1333 AD, are false teachers who totally control the NC.
4. The Iron/Clay Kingdom: This Kingdom marks the spiritual return of Jesus to the NC to remove the authority of the false teachers to rule over God's people. For the remainder of the NC, some of the rulers over the people of God will be like steel and follow Jesus, while others have no strength or integrity, and so, are like clay (Daniel 2:33). It will be a divided kingdom with a fractured mess of numerous Christian faith denominations who will reign side by side from 1333–2333 AD.
5. The Rock: This fifth ruler over the people of God came "in the time of those Kings," between the Silver and Bronze Kingdoms in 33 AD (Daniel 2:34–35). It is the "stone that struck the image" to become "a great mountain that filled the whole earth." Jesus, the Rock Kingdom, will rule forever.

2. NEBUCHADNEZZAR'S VISION OF A GREAT TREE (DANIEL 4:10–16)

Nebuchadnezzar was referred to as the Gold Kingdom reign because of this vision that provides BOTH a summary of that King's redemption AND the redemption for all people through Jesus. Nebuchadnezzar represented Jesus, and through his second vision, we learn that his life described the mission of Jesus, too. Jesus is the tree of life that came to the world so that "all flesh was fed from it" (Daniel 4:10–12). But the ruthless false teachers of the Bronze Kingdom cut down the tree because they wanted the NC for themselves (Daniel 4:13–14). The foundation of Jesus as the stump and roots of the tree remained "even with a band of iron and bronze," signifying the mixed Iron/Clay Kingdom (Daniel 4:15). With seven indicating something complete, Jesus' Kingdom will last forever, "let seven times pass over him" (Daniel 4:16).

3. DANIEL'S VISION OF THE BEASTS (DANIEL 7:4–14)

The first beast is representative of Jesus as God who came to the world in the form of a man who was referred to as the lion of the tribe of Judah (Daniel 7:4). The second beast is Satan who came to the world to destroy the NC and keep people from being redeemed through the blood of Jesus (Daniel 7:5). The third beast was representative of false teachers who took control of the NC and forced their will on the people of God (Daniel 7:6). The third beast appointed a fourth beast to speak for them (Daniel 7:7–8). They claimed to speak for God and persecuted and executed anyone who objected to their power and control over the people of God throughout the time of the NC. But Jesus reigns over all, and the corruption of the NC will end with judgment (Daniel 7:9–10). The first half of the NC of Jesus will be ruled by the two beasts who claim to speak for God but then God will take away their authority to rule over the people of God (Daniel 7:11), but their effects on the NC will continue through the second half of the NC—the mixed kingdom (Daniel 7:12) that started when Jesus returned (Daniel 7:13). The Kingdom of Jesus will last forever (Daniel 7:14).

4. DANIEL'S VISION OF THE RAM AND THE GOAT (DANIEL 8:3–12)

Daniel 8:3–8, explained by Daniel from 8:20–22, describes the Silver Kingdom from the statue of Nebuchadnezzar, which occurs during the OC. Therefore, I will fast forward to the time of Jesus that is addressed through the remainder of the vision. Out of the OC came a group of Jewish leaders who created a rigid system of religious rules (Daniel 8:8). They were very powerful when Jesus came, and they trampled on him and his followers and took away the sacrifice of Jesus and replaced it with themselves—the AOD (Daniel 8:9–12).

Then Daniel hears two men talking about specific times in the vision:

> [13] Then I heard a holy one speaking; and another holy one said to that certain one who spoke, "How long will the vision about the continual burnt offering, and the disobedience that makes desolate, to give both the sanctuary and the army to be trodden under foot be?" [14] He said to me, "To two thousand and three hundred evenings and mornings. Then the sanctuary will be cleansed." (Daniel 8:13–14)

The two men Daniel hears having a conversation are talking about the NC portion of the vision—the time from the AOD to when "the sanctuary will be cleansed." As you have seen through every vision of Daniel and through the first portion of Revelation, the sanctuary started out pure with Jesus, then was immediately corrupted, and will remain that way. Even when Jesus makes his spiritual return, the NC will be a mixed kingdom of corruption. It will remain affected by false teachers until the eternal kingdom of Jesus. In other words, Daniel hears two men talking about the hour of Jesus, the length of time of the NC.

Daniel learns it will be 2300 "evenings and mornings," and that term is like the term God used for creation, "evening and there was morning" (Genesis 1:5, 8, 13, 19, 23, and 31). Note that there are only six "evenings and mornings" provided in Genesis, and seven are needed for completion. This is confirmation that there are 2300 'somethings' from the AOD until the eternal kingdom of Jesus and judgment. The 2300 'somethings' can't be days, so it must be years. Therefore, in summary, the NC will last 2300 years from the AOD, which took place in 33 AD, to the arrival of the eternal kingdom at the time of the end. The NC will end in 2333 AD (33 AD plus 2300 years). Per God's clock, the "hour" of the NC is equal to 2,300 years on earth.

Considering that Revelation 8:1 tells me that the second half of the NC, when Jesus makes his spiritual return, is "about half an hour," and 20:1–6 tells me the return of Jesus is 1000 years long. Using God's math, with one half hour equal to 1000 years, the second half of the NC is equal to 26 minutes (=1000/2300*60 minutes) of heaven time. With the last half of the NC 1,000 years long, the first half must be 1300 years long (2300 years-1000 years). The first half of the NC with the false teachers in control of the NC is also about half an hour, so it is equal to 34 minutes of heaven time (=1300/2300*60 minutes). The transition between the first and second halves of the hour of the NC happened in 1333 AD.

5. DANIEL'S VISION OF THE SEVENTY SEVENS (DANIEL 9:24–27)

On behalf of Israel, Daniel prayed to God for an answer to the end of their punishment for sin and rebellion against God (Daniel 9:1–23). God responded to that prayer with Daniel 9:24–27, the most perfect and complete prophecy for the Messiah ever presented. What seems like a very short answer is packed full of prophecy describing the replacement of the daily sacrifice required under the Law with a one-time Messiah sacrifice. The transition to the NC is described in full:

> "Seventy weeks are decreed on your people and on your holy city, to finish disobedience, to make an end of sins, to make reconciliation for iniquity, to bring in everlasting righteousness, to seal up vision and prophecy, and to anoint the most holy." (Daniel 9:24)

Daniel is told that the process of redemption for God's people for the forgiveness of their sin is a decree of seventy weeks. A week is seven days, and a seven, mentioned thirty-six times in Revelation, is something that is complete. Therefore, the "seventy weeks" of Daniel 9:24 can also be considered 'seventy sevens,' and this is a term frequently used by scholars.

Daniel had asked God about the redemption of God's people, and God pointed Daniel straight to the Messiah. There are three portions to the seventy sevens:

1. People will be made forever right with God through the forgiveness of their sin,
2. Visions of prophecy will end, and,
3. The Messiah will be anointed.

The next three verses provide the details of those three aspects of the seventy sevens. First, there are two groups of sevens described:

> "Know therefore and discern that from the going out of the commandment to restore and build Jerusalem to the Anointed One, the prince, will be seven weeks and sixty-two weeks. It will be built again, with street and moat, even in troubled times." (Daniel 9:25)

The prophecy specifically states that Jerusalem will be restored AND built, not rebuilt. This is a promise for rebuilding the existing destroyed Jerusalem AND building the Holy City as Jesus. Jesus will REPLACE the temple of worship in Jerusalem. Jesus is the New Jerusalem, and this is confirmed to be an eternal promise:

> I saw the holy city, New Jerusalem, coming down out of heaven from God, prepared like a bride adorned for her husband. (Revelation 21:2)

A command will come for Jesus as the replacement of the place of worship, and we were told in Daniel 9:24 that after that command, prophecy will go silent. Therefore, the starting point must be the last prophecy that will inform the world about building Jerusalem through Jesus. The second event is "to the anointed one," the birth of the Messiah. Both the 'seven sevens' and the 'sixty-two sevens' will occur between those two decreed events.

Sixty-two sevens is equal to 434 years, and Malachi 3:1–3 is the last OT prophecy of the Messiah before visions and prophecy went silent. Since Jesus' birth is estimated to have been 6 BC, going back 434 years from that date calculates the year that Malachi received that last vision prophecy. The year 440 BC matches the range of scholars' estimates for the year Malachi's prophecy was written. Also, during this time, there will be 'seven sevens.' With a seven being something complete, the 'seven sevens' is a reference to the most complete entity that ever existed, so this must be a reference to Jesus. Jesus always existed, so between Malachi's prophecy and the birth of Jesus, both the 'sixty-two sevens' and the 'seven sevens' occurred. Daniel 9:24–25 has been met through the existence and birth of Jesus.

The next verse provides details of what will happen to Jesus after he comes:

> After the sixty-two weeks, the Anointed One will be cut off, and will have nothing. The people of the prince who come will destroy the city and the sanctuary. Its end will be with a flood, and war will be even to the end. Desolations are determined. (Daniel 9:26)

Sometime after Jesus comes, he will have no possessions, and he will be executed. We know that Jesus came into the world at the end of the sixty-two weeks in 6 BC, and with his crucifixion in 30 AD with him having no possessions as recorded in the Gospels, Jesus fulfilled that first portion of Daniel 9:26. We've already been through the Olivet Discourse, the first half of Revelation prophecy and a few visions in Daniel that all tell us that the NC will be immediately attacked then controlled by false teachers working with Satan. The new Jerusalem through Jesus will be destroyed, and "war will be even to the end." The destruction and takeover of the NC will be fast, complete, and there will be a fight for its ownership until the end.

The last verse provides a critical piece of data that will validate the testimony of Jesus' eyewitnesses:

> "He will make a firm covenant with many for one week. In the middle of the week, he will cause the sacrifice and the offering to cease. On the wing of abominations will come one who makes desolate; and even to the decreed full end, wrath will be poured out on the desolate." (Daniel 9:27)

Jesus as the Messiah will have a seven-year mission, and in the middle of those seven years, he will become the permanent sacrifice for sin that eliminates the daily sacrifice requirement. Jesus' mission started in 26 AD and lasted seven years until 33 AD. He was executed in the middle of his mission, and this matches scholars' estimates of Jesus' crucifixion occurring in 30 AD. Jesus promised his eyewitnesses that he would not leave them orphans, and he didn't—he breathed the Holy Spirit into them, so Jesus remained with them for the second half of his mission from 30–33 AD, while they documented their testimony for all future nations. The last point to be made is that God promised to pour out his wrath on those responsible for the AOD.

6. DANIEL'S VISION OF THE FUTURE OF THE PEOPLE OF GOD (DANIEL 10:5—12:13)

This vision, with a lot of complex details, is very long because it addresses the OC and the NC. Like the others, it has a chronological element to it, and since I am only interested in the evidence package for Jesus, I will separate the OC vision portion from the NC evidence. Knowing this, there is one section that I can be certain will take me straight to the NC, the AOD:

> [31] "Forces from him will profane the sanctuary, even the fortress, and will take away the continual burnt offering. Then they will set up the abomination that makes desolate. [32] He will corrupt those who do wickedly against the covenant by flatteries; but the people who know their God will be strong and take action. (Daniel 11:31–32)

The newly built Jerusalem, the NC, will be attacked, and Jesus' sacrifice will be owned by others. False teachers will persecute the disciples who provided their testimony of Jesus and will claim ownership of the NC. They will "set up" the AOD, which is the worst thing that could happen to those seeking redemption, because false teachers with Satan have replaced the NC with themselves. Instead of the living water and the bread of life, the message for the first half of the NC will be wickedness, sin, and corruption. The people of God will fight back, but it will result in the executions of many of them (Daniel 11:33–35). False teachers will claim to speak for God, and they will turn the NC into a haven for dishonesty, profit, and control of property and wealth (Daniel 11:36–39).

War will continue for control of the NC up to the time of the end when the wrath of God is poured out on those supporting evil (Daniel 11:40–45). The time of the end will be the worst time ever to be experienced throughout history, and the few remaining followers of Jesus will be killed (Daniel 12:1). Then it will be time for judgment and those whose names are in the book of life will be rewarded with everlasting life, but those whose names are missing will find everlasting contempt (Daniel 12:2–3). The book of life will be kept private until the end, meaning nobody is able to determine the fate of another person (Daniel 12:4).

Then, in closing, Daniel hears another conversation between two men (Daniel 12:5–6), and one of them asks, "How long will it be to the end of these wonders?" The wonders described are the redemption of people with their names in the book of life:

> [7] I heard the man clothed in linen, who was above the waters of the river, when he held up his right hand and his left hand to heaven, and swore by him who lives forever that it will be for a time, times, and a half; and when they have finished breaking in pieces the power of the holy people, all these things will be finished. (Daniel 12:7)

It will be a "time, times, and a half" for redemption, then the NC will be broken into pieces. Afterwards, the end will come. Daniel claimed he didn't understand the discussion and was told that the meaning is "sealed until the time of the end" (Daniel 12:8–9). Note that John stated that the last time, the time of the end, will be the hour of Jesus (1 John 2:18–19); therefore, the answer is not sealed up forever, it was sealed up until the NC. The solution to "a time, times, and a half" will be found when Jesus has arrived and set up his kingdom.

We find a redemption connection of Daniel's "a time, times, and a half," given to John in a vision near the start of the NC:

> The woman was given the two wings of a great eagle, so that she might fly to the place prepared for her in the wilderness, where she would be taken care of for a time, times, and half a time, out of the serpent's reach. (Revelation 12:14)

Revelation has provided an answer to "a time, times, and a half" that explains the redemption of the people of God. The first half of Jesus' mission was protected by God as presented in Revelation 12:6, and the second half of Jesus' mission, which will be "a time, times and half a time," will also be protected by God. The second half of Jesus' mission is the documenting of Jesus' testimony that will be the path to redemption for all people of the future.

The message will be that many will follow the Good News of Jesus documented in the testimony of Jesus' chosen eyewitnesses and will get their names written in the book of life, but the wicked won't understand (Daniel 12:10). Then Daniel provided you the exact number of days that the "time, times, and a half" will be for the Good News to be documented:

> 11 "From the time that the continual burnt offering is taken away and the abomination that makes desolate set up, there will be one thousand two hundred ninety days. (Daniel 12:11)

From the time between the "continual burnt offering is taken away," and "the abomination that makes desolate set up," the AOD, there will be 1290 days. The continual burnt offering requirement ended with Jesus' one-time sacrifice—it was no longer required. The false teachers started the AOD the day the Good News was documented—the same day of the start of the great tribulation in 33 AD. Therefore, there were 1290 days from Jesus' sacrifice to the start of the great persecution—the day the eyewitnesses completed their testimony. The second half of Jesus' seven-year mission will last 1290 days. This ends the evidence for Jesus from Daniel, but it connects directly to the next section of Revelation that will build on the math presented thus far.

The next verse in Daniel is very important, but the analysis of it will have to wait for the analysis of the resurrection events of Jesus because it is connected to the last half of Jesus' mission, the 1,290 days, and Jesus' forty days of appearances:

> Blessed is he who waits, and comes to the one thousand three hundred thirty-five days. (Daniel 12:12)

I'll keep you waiting in anticipation for that result.

DANIEL PROPHECY JESUS EVIDENCE

1. Jesus is God born as a man with a mission to start the NC (6 BC)
    a. Daniel 2:32, 44—Jesus born, lived, and completed his mission during in the Silver Kingdom (562 BC-33 AD), with some rulers Godly and others following evil

b. Daniel 4:10–12—Jesus is the tree of life that came to the world so that "all flesh was fed from it"

c. Daniel 7:4, 14—Jesus has everlasting dominion with a permanent Kingdom

d. Daniel 9:25—There were "sixty-two sevens," 434 years from the last Messiah prophecy Malachi 3:1–3 to Jesus' birth, who as the "seven sevens" always existed

e. Revelation 21:2—Jesus is the "New Jerusalem," the replacement of the OC with the NC with a Kingdom that will last forever

2. Satan attempted to stop the NC from starting (6 BC)

   a. Daniel 7:5—The second beast is Satan who came to the world to destroy the NC and keep people from being redeemed through the blood of Jesus

   b. Daniel 8:8—Out of the OC came a powerful group of Jewish leaders who formed their own religion with rules and regulations that didn't come from God

3. Jesus' mission to teach, heal and perform miracles (26–30 AD)

   a. Daniel 9:27—The first half of Jesus' seven-year mission to have his chosen eyewitnesses observe him teach and perform works to prove he was the Messiah

4. Jesus' sacrifice and resurrection (30 AD)

   a. Daniel 9:27—As the replacement for the Holy City, Jesus' permanent sin sacrifice in the middle of his seven-year mission, made people forever righteous

5. Second half of Jesus' seven-year mission (30–33 AD)

   a. Daniel 9:27—The second half of Jesus' seven-year mission, to give his chosen eyewitnesses the Holy Spirit of God to help them complete their testimony

   b. Daniel 12:7—The testimony of Jesus' eyewitnesses will save many and it will happen during a "time, times and half a time"

   c. Daniel 12:10–11—The "time, times, and half a time" correspond to the 1,290 days between when the daily sacrifice is abolished and the abomination that causes desolation

6. Start of the NC, Great Tribulation, and the Testimonies are completed (33 AD)
    a. Daniel 4:16–17—With seven indicating something complete, Jesus' Kingdom will last forever, "let seven times pass over him"
    b. Daniel 9:26–27—The false teachers with Satan will commit the AOD that will replace Jesus' permanent sacrifice with themselves claiming to speak for God
    c. Daniel 11:31–32 –False teachers with Satan replace Jesus NC with themselves, referred to as the AOD
7. Generation of the Disciples (33–67 AD)
8. The NC (33–2333 AD)
    a. Daniel 2:34–35—Jesus is the rock that came in the Silver/Bronze Kingdom interface to replace all other rulers over the people of God during the NC; it will last forever
    b. Daniel 7:6–8—The third beast, the bronze rulers, were given dominion given from God to reign over the people of God, and they appointed a fourth beast, and their corruption will last throughout the NC
    c. Daniel 8:8–14—The religious leaders who trampled on Jesus and his disciples took away Jesus' sacrifice through their AOD, and corrupted the 2300 years of the NC
    d. Daniel 9:26–27—The false teachers and Satan will destroy the NC to the end of time when those responsible will have the wrath of God poured out on them
9. First half of the NC—the reign of the Beast (33–1333 AD)
    a. Daniel 2:32, 39—The Bronze Kingdom false teachers who took control of the NC by claiming to speak for Jesus rule over the people of God
    b. Daniel 4:13–14—Ruthless false teachers claiming to be God during the Bronze Kingdom cut down the tree because they wanted the NC for themselves
    c. Daniel 7:11—The two beasts rule over the people of God with an iron fist as they claim to be able to speak for God

   d. Daniel 11:33–39—False teachers use Jesus' sanctuary for profit, control of property, and wealth; some followers of Jesus will fight back and lose their lives

10. Second half of Jesus' NC—Jesus' 1000-year reign with his chosen ones (1333–2333 AD)
    a. Daniel 2:33, 40–43—A mixed Kingdom of Iron and Clay with a fractured mess of numerous Christian faith denominations, who will reign side by side throughout
    b. Daniel 4:15—Jesus as the stump and roots of the tree remained "even with a band of iron and bronze," signifying the Iron/Clay Kingdom with the return of Jesus
    c. Daniel 7:12–13—God took away the beasts' authority, and Jesus returned to rule over God's mixed people, with some following God and others following evil
    d. Daniel 11:40–45—The battle between the people of God and Satan for the NC will last until the end of time
11. The Time of the End (2333-?)
    a. Daniel 12:1—The time of the end will be a miserable existence
12. Judgement
    a. Daniel 7:9–10—Jesus has an eternal kingdom, and the NC will end in judgment for those who corrupted it
    b. Daniel 12:1–4—Those with their name in the book of life will be rewarded, and those left out will feel everlasting contempt

11

The Woman of Revelation

IN THIS LAST PORTION of prophecy, I'll be examining Revelation 12:1—16:21 to provide additional details and evidence for the NC from the start to the end. It's the same story told with different visuals. Through the depiction of the NC as a "woman," God protected Jesus and his eyewitnesses from harm throughout Jesus' life and mission. In chapter twelve of Revelation, the NC, as the woman, starts out with Jesus pure, but by the time false teachers and Satan are through with her, she is sinister, evil, and a haven for sin. From later in Revelation, there is a depiction of the transformed woman.

> [3] He carried me away in the Spirit into a wilderness. I saw a woman sitting on a scarlet-colored beast, full of blasphemous names, having seven heads and ten horns. [4] The woman was dressed in purple and scarlet, and decked with gold and precious stones and pearls, having in her hand a golden cup full of abominations and the impurities of the sexual immorality of the earth. [5] And on her forehead a name was written, "MYSTERY, BABYLON THE GREAT, THE MOTHER OF THE PROSTITUTES AND OF THE ABOMINATIONS OF THE EARTH." [6] I saw the woman drunken with the blood of the saints and with the blood of the martyrs of Jesus. When I saw her, I wondered with great amazement. (Revelation 17:3–6)

I presented a description of what became of the woman because I thought it helpful to know in advance the vivid details God provides to describe the corruption and sin that affected God's redemption plan. I say "affected" because most of it is in the past.

Think of all the various denominations and wealth associated with the Christian church, and you can visualize the many NC churches that focus on the business of peddling their religious message of Jesus for profit. The AOD in 33 AD is the source of these abominations—the founders of the Catholic Church and originators of NC corruption who are referred to as the "MOTHER OF THE PROSTITUTES." But don't take my word for it, read this account in Revelation that has Jesus presenting the complete details of the NC future to John, the disciple whom Jesus loved.

God in heaven planned the transition of the OC to the NC through a virgin giving birth to Jesus, who with twelve disciples would fulfill Daniel 9:24–27 prophecy (Revelation 12:1–2). But Satan, with a great following, was intent on eliminating the NC before it even started (Revelation 12:3–5). Satan failed to eliminate the child Jesus in his youth (Matthew 1:18- 2:20). The child grew, then it was on to his seven-year mission to start the NC, which, during the first half, God protected Jesus and his disciples:

> The woman fled into the wilderness to a place prepared for her by God, where she might be taken care of for 1,260 days. (Revelation 12:6).

For 1260 days, God protected the disciples with Jesus as he taught, healed, and performed miracles.

During this decreed 1260-day period, Satan with his followers again attempted to prevent Jesus from completing his mission to start the NC, referred to as the "hour" of Jesus, but the time of the NC had not yet come:

> They sought, therefore, to take him; but no one laid a hand on him, because his hour had not yet come (John 7:30)

> Jesus spoke these words in the treasury, as he taught in the temple. Yet no one arrested him, because his hour had not yet come. (John 8:20)

Remember the story of redemption in Daniel that was sealed until the end time that John stated was the final hour (1 John 2:18)? This hour is the NC, and through Revelation, Jesus, through John, is now providing you the exact details of the redemption plan for the people of God. Also, recall that the 1260 days for Jesus to preach and perform works were duplicated by Peter and Andrew as the two witnesses of Revelation 11:3.

Through God's protection of the disciples and Jesus, Satan failed to stop Jesus from completing his 1260-day mission, but the attacks of Satan were not through (Revelation 12:7–10). The disciples were determined to provide their testimony even to the point of death because they believed in the blood of Jesus that was shed for them (Revelation 12:11). Once the testimony of Jesus' eyewitnesses was completed, there would be no stopping the NC from being born. Therefore, Satan knew he only had a short time to stop the disciples from providing the foundation of the NC—their testimony (Revelation 12:12–13). But God protected Jesus' eyewitnesses so they could finish their testimony that would spread the Good News throughout the world (Mark 13:10):

> Two wings of the great eagle were given to the woman, that she might fly into the wilderness to her place, so that she might be nourished for a time, times, and half a time, from the face of the serpent. (Revelation 12:14)

Recall that the "times, time, and half a time" in Revelation 12:14 is connected to Daniel 12:7–11 to define the length of time of God's protection. Based on that connection, we found that from the time the daily sacrifice was abolished through Jesus' sacrifice until the start of the AOD, there will be 1290 days.

The plan of redemption for all the people of the world was decreed to come through the testimony of the eyewitnesses of Jesus, who God protected for 1290 days. This is the second half of Jesus' seven-year mission, and it was completed as decreed by God. Jesus and his disciples were protected for the entire seven-year mission of Jesus—1260 days, then a sacrifice in the middle, then 1290 days. In other words, Jesus' seven-year mission equaled:

1,260 days for teaching/works + days of Jesus' sacrifice +1,290 days for testimony documentation

Less the days of the sacrifice of Jesus, there are 2,550 days accounted for Jesus' seven-year mission.

There are exactly 365.25 days in a year; therefore, the seven-year mission of Jesus had exactly 365.25 x 7 days in it, which totals 2556.75 days. The sacrifice of Jesus in the middle must have taken 6.75 days (2556.75–2550=6.75). Through a bit of analysis, John the disciple told us the exact number of days of Jesus' sacrifice:

1. Jesus was anointed as the Passover lamb by Mary Magdalene six days before Passover (John 12:1–3). The anointing occurred at "supper" or "dinner."
2. Jesus' sacrifice on the Preparation Day—the day before the Passover (John 19:31).

3. Jesus was placed in the tomb the same day he was executed so that he wouldn't remain on the cross during the Sabbath, the Saturday that was the next day, and in this case was also the Passover (John 19:31).
4. Jesus was then resurrected on the first day of the week—the day after Passover (John 20:1), which was also Sunday.

Therefore, a breakdown of the official days of Jesus' sacrifice is:

- Portion of a day—Sunday—At suppertime, Jesus is anointed as the sacrifice 6 days before Passover Day (John 12:1–3)
- Full day—Monday—Jesus preparing for his sacrifice
- Full day—Tuesday—Jesus preparing for his sacrifice
- Full day—Wednesday—Jesus preparing for his sacrifice
- Full day—Thursday—Arrest and Trial
- Full day—Friday—Jesus executed as the sacrifice on Preparation Day and placed in the tomb late that day (John 19:42)
- Full day—Saturday—Sabbath and Passover Day; Jesus is in the tomb
- Portion of a day—Sunday—Resurrection Day, Jesus first appeared to Mary sometime after the tomb was found empty that morning (John 20:14)

As Jesus promised, he rose on the third day (Mark 9:31). Jesus' sacrifice was six full days plus two portions of days, equaling three-quarters of a day. Jesus' sacrifice in summary took a total of 6.75 days.

Together with the number of days in the two halves of Jesus' mission, we have the exact number of days of Jesus' seven-year mission, 1,260 + 6.75 + 1,290 = 2556.75 days. God provided perfect math in prophecy, telling you the exact days of each portion of Jesus' seven-year mission as described several hundred years in advance in Daniel 9:24–27.

But the story is far from over. After the protected seven-year mission of Jesus ended, Satan, with the false teachers, came to bring their AOD:

> [15] The serpent spewed water out of his mouth after the woman, like a river, that he might cause her to be carried away by the stream. [16] The earth helped the woman, and the earth opened its mouth and swallowed up the river which the dragon spewed out of his mouth. [17] The dragon grew angry with the woman, and went away to make

> war with the rest of her offspring, who keep God's commandments and hold Jesus' testimony. (Revelation 12:15–17)

Immediately after Jesus' eyewitnesses completed their testimony, false teachers working and speaking for Satan infiltrated the disciples who were commissioning the NC. The people of the earth joined forces with Satan to claim they speak for God, and through that claim, intimidation, and force, they took total control of the NC. This war did not end with the disciples, because anyone following Jesus and the testimony of his eyewitnesses was attacked.

The woman, the NC, was transformed from being pure to something that was evil and was controlled by Satan. Jesus now referred to them as a beast (Revelation 13:1–10)—the third beast of Daniel. The beast, as the self-proclaimed spokesperson for God, stopped at nothing to control every aspect of the NC and even society. They persecuted, executed, and spread so that ALL people worshipped the beast. The beast was given a mouth to utter proud words and blasphemies, and to exercise its authority to make war for forty-two months (Revelation 13:5). The forty-two months connect the beast to those who persecuted and executed the two witnesses (Revelation11:1–3).

Then a second beast came out of the first beast to be the official and designated spokesman for the first beast (Revelation 13:11–17). We are told how the beasts came about through the following descriptions of the two beasts:

> One of the heads of the beast seemed to have had a fatal wound, but the fatal wound had been healed. The whole world was filled with wonder and followed the beast. (Revelation 13:3)

> Because of the signs it was given power to perform on behalf of the first beast, it deceived the inhabitants of the earth. It ordered them to set up an image in honor of the beast who was wounded by the sword and yet lived. (Revelation 13:14)

The beast used the name of one of the two witnesses they executed to take total control of the woman. Andrew AND Peter were the two witnesses, but the beast chose to use the name of Peter to own the woman. Peter was a prime candidate for the false teacher coup of the NC because Peter was vocal, so he was frequently mentioned in the eyewitness testimony—the Gospels.

There is no doubt that Peter became the path for the coup of the NC because the beast still claims this:

> Catechism #880—When Christ instituted the Twelve, "he constituted [them] in the form of a college or permanent assembly, at the head of which he placed Peter, chosen from among them."[398] Just as "by the Lord's institution, St. Peter and the rest of the apostles constitute a single apostolic college, so in like fashion the Roman Pontiff, Peter's successor, and the bishops, the successors of the apostles, are related with and united to one another."[399]

This evidence comes straight from the Catholic Church's operating manual, which they refer to as their Catechism (English translation of the Catechism of the Catholic Church for the United States of America, © 1994). Yes, the Catechism is a recent document, but I don't think anyone can dispute the claims of the Catholic Church to have originated in the very early days of the church through Jesus' commissioning Peter to lead it. Their strategy to maintain control of the woman may have morphed over the years, but history proves them to be the beast that took control of the woman. Note that the mark of the beast, referred to as "666" (Revelation 13:18), is representative of those who reject Jesus to follow the beast. There is much debate about what "666" refers to, and personally, because God knows the future, I think it is represented by the following verse:

> At this, many of his disciples went back and walked no more with him. (John 6:66)

Taking the focus off Jesus to worship the beasts will result in eternal death.

The beasts ruthlessly ruled for many years until the decreed number of those who refused to follow the beast, 144000, were executed (Revelation 14:1–5). The martyrs were those who "were not defiled with women, for they are virgins." The woman is the beast, and the martyrs rejected the maddening wine and advances of the beast. They were virgins because they didn't partake in the sins of the woman. The chosen ones were those who were determined to "follow the Lamb wherever he goes," even to their death.

Then this portion of Revelation notes the transition from the reign of the beasts to the return of Jesus to the NC:

> I saw an angel flying in mid heaven, having an eternal Good News to proclaim to those who dwell on the earth—to every nation, tribe, language, and people. (Revelation 14:6)

At the decreed time, the Good News will no longer be controlled by the beasts because Jesus returned to the NC and removed the beast's authority to control the woman. Jesus facilitated the spread of the Good News throughout the world, and God promised to punish the beast (Revelation 14:7). The reign of the beast ended, but they continue to persuade people to follow them rather than Jesus. But God warned that those following the beast will also be punished (Revelation 14:8–11). As expected, in the second half hour of the NC, those who die in the Lord will be blessed and rewarded (Revelation 14:12–13). Those who followed the beast will see Jesus and realize their fate with the wrath of God being poured out on them (Revelation 14:14–20).

The second half of the NC will end with Jesus returning to heaven, which is once again open for business:

> [5] After these things, I looked, and the temple of the tabernacle of the testimony in heaven was opened. [6] The seven angels who had the seven plagues came out, clothed with pure, bright linen, and wearing golden sashes around their chests. (Revelation 15:5–6)

Jesus is back in heaven, but it's time for the wrath of God to be poured out on the earth—the beast—from seven bowls (Revelation 15:1—16:1). During this time of the end, the world is darkened because the light of Jesus has been removed from the earth, and those worshiping the beast are punished with sickness and war (Revelation 16:2–16).

Finally, the seventh trumpet brings the turmoil of the sights and sounds of war facing anyone left alive by the previous bowls of God's wrath (Revelation 16:17–19). John confirms that the mountains symbolizing where God meets his people no longer exist because there are no followers of Jesus remaining in the world (Revelation 16:20). The bombing in his vision is not a pretty sight:

> [20] Every island fled away, and the mountains were not found. [21] Great hailstones, about the weight of a talent, came down out of the sky on people. People blasphemed God because of the plague of the hail, for this plague was exceedingly severe. (Revelation 16:20–21)

John described "Great hailstones" because he had never seen a bomb. The final chapters of Revelation provide more details of the punishment of those who rejected Jesus to follow the beast, and then provide a description of the change of the NC to the eternal kingdom of Jesus. I'll leave those details and analysis to you, as the evidence package for Jesus is already overwhelming and complete.

MORE REVELATION JESUS EVIDENCE

1. Jesus is God born as a man with a mission to start the NC (6 BC)
    a. Revelation 12:1–2—God sent a Messiah to the world to start the NC that is referred to in Revelation as a "woman"
2. Satan attempted to stop the NC from starting (6 BC)
    a. Revelation 12:3–5—Very early in Jesus' life, Satan, with a great following, attempted to stop Jesus' seven-year mission from happening to start the NC, but Satan failed
    b. Matthew 1:18—2:20—Satan failed to eliminate and stop Jesus
3. Jesus' mission to teach, heal and perform miracles (26–30 AD)
    a. Revelation 12:6—God protected Jesus and his eyewitness disciples for 1260 days—Jesus' mission days are equal to the 1260 days the two witnesses testified for Jesus
    b. Revelation 12:7–10—Satan, working with false teachers, continues their attacks on Jesus, but through the blood of Jesus, his disciples overcame evil to testify
4. Jesus' sacrifice and resurrection (30 AD)
    a. Revelation 12:11—Jesus' disciples triumphed over Satan and the false teachers by witnessing Jesus' sacrifice, so that they will testify even to death
    b. John 12:1–3, 19:31,42, 20:1, 14—Together, these passages prove Jesus' sacrifice is exactly 6.75 days
    c. Mark 9:31—Jesus' promise to rise on the third day has been fulfilled
5. Second half of Jesus' seven-year mission (30–33 AD)
    a. Revelation 12:12–13—Satan knew he only had a short time to attack Jesus' chosen disciples to prevent their testimony from being documented to start the NC
    b. Revelation 12:14—God protected the eyewitness disciples from harm for a "time, times, and half a time," which is about 3–1/2 years, and correlates to 1290 days

c. Daniel 12:7—The words a "time, times, and a half" correlate to Revelation 12:14

d. Daniel 12:10–11—With God's protection between Jesus' sacrifice and the AOD, there are exactly 1290 days decreed for the disciples to document their testimony

e. John 12:1–3, 19:31, 42, and 20:1, 14—Jesus' sacrifice is exactly 6.75 days long

f. Daniel 9:27—Through Revelation 12:14, Daniel 12:7, 10–11, and words of John, the decreed seven-year mission of Jesus to start the NC is proven exactly 2556.75 days

6. Start of the NC, the Great Tribulation, and the AOD (33 AD)

   a. Revelation 12:15–16—Immediately after God's protection of the disciples ceased, false teachers claimed to be God, and followers of evil agreed

   b. Revelation 12:17—Satan and the false teachers made war with the followers of Jesus

7. Generation of the Disciples (33–67 AD)

   a. Revelation 13:1–10—Jesus refers to the false teachers together with Satan as the beast who persecutes and executes anyone who doesn't accept their reign

   b. Revelation 13:11–17—Another beast comes out of the first beast to speak on their behalf

   c. Revelation 13:3, 14—The beasts took their authority from Peter, one of the two witnesses they executed

   d. Revelation 13:5—42 months of persecution connect the beast to Peter, one of the two witnesses of Revelation 11:1–3, as the beast's path to possess the woman

8. The NC (33–2333 AD)

   a. Revelation 17:3–6—The false teachers who Jesus called the "beasts" and "The Mother of the Prostitutes and of the Abominations of the Earth," corrupted the NC

   b. John 7:30, 8:20—The NC is an hour long per the eternal clock

9. First half of the NC—the reign of the Beast (33–1333 AD)
    a. Revelation 13:1–17—The beasts persecuted and executed everyone who objected to their NC authority and reign, and forced everyone to worship them
    b. Revelation 14:1–5—The beast executed 144,000 blameless followers of Jesus who were virgins because they rejected the sinful woman
10. Second half of Jesus' NC—Jesus' 1000-year reign with his chosen ones (1333–2333 AD)
    a. Revelation 14:6 –Jesus returned to free the Good News from the beasts and removed their authority to rule over the NC; they no longer rule, but they aren't eliminated
    b. Revelation 14:7–20—Jesus warns people to make the right choice and reject the beast to be blessed, or follow the beast to face the wrath of God and be punished
11. The Time of the End (2333-?)
    a. Revelation 13:18—The "666" connects those following the beast to John 6:66 as those who reject Jesus and are judged and condemned
    b. Revelation 15:1—16:1—At the time of the end, the last part of the second half of the NC, God will pour seven bowls of wrath out on those who follow the beasts
    c. Revelation 16:2–16—God pours out six bowls of wrath on the beast, then Jesus warns that he will return like the thief in the night to end Satan's war on Jesus
    d. Revelation 16:17–21—The end is described with no followers of Jesus left on the earth, and large hailstones representing bombs destroy the world
12. Judgement

12

The Christian Religious Leader Theology Package

From prophecy, we know that Jesus provided a very thorough evidence package meant to prove Jesus to the world through eyewitness testimony. The evidence package provided by God through prophecy explains how the evidence package for Jesus was put together by the disciples, then describes in detail what happened to it. I've already stated that CRLs claim the Gospels were written many years after Jesus and that the ECFs stated that the authors were unknown, so they helped us out by naming them. This does not match what God told us to expect.

We don't have two- or three-eyewitness testimonies from those Jesus chose; we have an ECF and CRL-developed theological package. Luke is not eyewitness testimony, and the words of Paul and all letters except those from John are not the word of God. Therefore, what I am left with is three of the four Gospels that have the potential for being eyewitness testimony of Jesus, and their names came from ECFs rather than being documented in the books. The ECF descriptions of the Gospel authors and their dates of origin are not backed up with evidence; therefore, the theological package provided by the CRLs appears to be useless.

But I need a starting point to get to the truth, so the first step is to take a closer look at the three potential eyewitness testimonies for an overall high-level quick evaluation. Starting with the book claimed to be written by Matthew, who is listed as one of the twelve disciples in the Gospels of Matthew and Mark, the author is named Matthew, one of the twelve.

> [2] Now the names of the twelve apostles are these. The first, Simon, who is called Peter; Andrew, his brother; James the son of Zebedee; John, his brother; [3] Philip; Bartholomew; Thomas; Matthew the tax collector; James the son of Alphaeus; Lebbaeus, who was also called Thaddaeus; [4] Simon the Zealot; and Judas Iscariot, who also betrayed him. (Matthew 10:2–4)

> [16] Simon (to whom he gave the name Peter); [17] James the son of Zebedee; and John, the brother of James, (whom he called Boanerges, which means, Sons of Thunder); [18] Andrew; Philip; Bartholomew; Matthew; Thomas; James, the son of Alphaeus; Thaddaeus; Simon the Zealot; [19] and Judas Iscariot, who also betrayed him. (Mark 3:14–19)

Notice that the summary in Matthew doesn't tell you anything about the careers of eleven of the disciples, but it very clearly wants you to know that Matthew is "the tax collector." This is an odd point to make, considering that we know James, John, Peter, and Andrew to be fishermen, but we don't have information about the other disciples. I know that CRLs claim that this statement is in Matthew because that author is the tax collector, but that detail just seems to be too intentional, so I am questioning it.

Notice the similarities between the two accounts of the twelve disciples in Matthew and Mark ("James the son of Zebedee," "James the son of Alphaeus, "and "Judas Iscariot, who also betrayed him."). There are enough similarities to indicate that Matthew's author copied the list of the twelve from Mark's author. But there IS NO MENTION OF MATTHEW BEING A TAX COLLECTOR IN THE ORIGINAL VERSION. This is not a surprise!

The two accounts of the tax collector account, from Matthew and Mark, are presented for comparison analysis:

> [9] As Jesus passed by from there, he saw a man called Matthew sitting at the tax collection office. He said to him, "Follow me." He got up and followed him. [10] As he sat in the house, behold, many tax collectors and sinners came and sat down with Jesus and his disciples. [11] When the Pharisees saw it, they said to his disciples, "Why does your teacher eat with tax collectors and sinners?" (Matthew 9:9–11)

> [13] He went out again by the seaside. All the multitude came to him, and he taught them. [14] As he passed by, he saw Levi, the son of Alphaeus, sitting at the tax office. He said to him, "Follow me." And he arose and followed him. [15] He was reclining at the table in

> his house, and many tax collectors and sinners sat down with Jesus and his disciples, for there were many, and they followed him. [16] The scribes and the Pharisees, when they saw that he was eating with the sinners and tax collectors, said to his disciples, "Why is it that he eats and drinks with tax collectors and sinners?" (Mark 2:13–16)

It again appears as though the event in Matthew is an edited copy of what is written in Mark. This observation is proven to be true because the author of Mark provides all the eyewitness details about the tax collector. For example, in the version presented in Mark:

- The location is by the seaside in Capernaum,
- A crowd came to Jesus and he taught them,
- The tax collector was the son of Alphaeus,
- Jesus and the tax collector went to Levi's house,
- The tax collector reclined at the table in Levi's house while Jesus and many tax collectors and sinners sat down with Jesus, and,
- Then, to top it off, the tax collector is called Levi instead of Matthew.

Original observational accounts will contain eyewitness details, and copies provided as second-hand accounts will typically lose some of those eyewitness details.

If Matthew were the author AND the tax collector, as the ECFs and CRLs claim, the account in Matthew of the tax collector is his story of how Jesus recruited him. If this were true, the eyewitness details would be presented in Matthew rather than Mark. For example, consider the details John provided for his recruitment by Jesus (John 1:29–42). John described numerous details about what happened when he and Andrew first followed Jesus.

The author of the Gospel of Matthew obviously copied the tax collector account from Mark's author, but somebody attempted to hide that fact, and from what prophecy told me, it wasn't the author. In summary, the author of Mark knew the tax collector, and the author of Matthew didn't, and the account in Matthew is an edited copy of what was presented in Mark.

John described the twelve disciples of Jesus more thoroughly than the other Gospel authors. John didn't record the story of the tax collector and never mentioned a man named Matthew or Levi as being one of the twelve. In other words, according to John, Matthew wasn't one of the twelve disciples of Jesus, and neither was the tax collector Levi. Jesus wanted everyone to follow him, and apparently, a tax collector did so because Mark's author provided us all the details of it—he just wasn't one of the twelve, and he wasn't named Matthew.

The ECFs who lived many years after Jesus may have told us the author of the Gospel of Matthew is Matthew the tax collector, but John, one of Jesus ' disciples, through one of his letters, 1 John 2:18–19, told us not to believe those who came after the disciples. The old saying in investigations is to trust but always verify. Based on what John stated and the results of the presented analysis, I can't find even one sliver of evidence that verifies Matthew as the author of the Gospel of Matthew.

Matthew failed the eyewitness testimony verification test, so it is on to the Gospel of Mark. Just as it was for Matthew, the ECFs stated that Mark was written by a man named John Mark, who wrote down the words of Peter. I found no historical data or Bible documentation that confirmed their claims. The author of the Gospel of Mark does not name himself nor his sources; therefore, there is no reason to believe that this claim from the ECFs is true either. Like the other Gospels, the experts claim the Gospel of Mark was written many years after Jesus lived, and this is not representative of reliable testimony either. *According to what has been presented to followers of Jesus by the ECFs and accepted by CRLs*, the book referred to as the Gospel of Mark also CANNOT be considered eyewitness testimony.

It's apparent that with only one Gospel remaining to be reviewed—the Gospel of John, there will not be enough eyewitness testimony to validate the CRL theological package they present for Jesus. The CRL package meant to prove Jesus to the world fails God's eyewitness requirements (Deuteronomy 17:6 and 19:15). Law requirements are not met, nor does the CRL package support Jesus' plan for an eyewitness testimony package to have been written between 30–33 AD.

This clearly wasn't the intention of God. In fact, it gets worse. According to Deuteronomy 18:18–22, if Jesus cannot be proven through two or three witnesses, God told the world NOT TO BELIEVE the story. In other words, if you believe the theological story presented by ECFs and CRLs, you are not following the directions presented by God in the Bible. By default, the Bible, as the infallible and inerrant word of God, tells the people of the world that they MUST reject the Jesus presented to you by ECFs and CRLs. No wonder CRLs stress faith to believe in Jesus rather than evidence, and atheists have such a field day disproving the existence of God and, most of all, the existence of Jesus as God. CRLs contradict themselves with their Bible claim, then ignore God's requirements in it.

Knowing that Jesus put a plan and process in place to develop reliable eyewitness testimony to prove Jesus to all future nations and people, the evidence package exists, but I need to prove it. The God of evidence in my life has assured me that the evidence package Jesus promised was prepared and delivered. Prophecy in the Olivet Discourse, Daniel, and Revelation all confirmed that Jesus' testimony was provided for all the people of the world, but then false teachers corrupted it. Finally, I know that there are four disciples that Jesus chose to be his eyewitnesses, and there are three Gospels. This isn't a bad start, but I have a lot of work ahead of me.

13

Searching for Jesus' Evidence Package

The best place to start to search for eyewitness testimony for Jesus is the Gospel of John, because although it is anonymous like the other Gospels, it is closest to identifying the author. The author twice claimed that the Gospel of John is his testimony:

> He who has seen has testified, and his testimony is true. He knows that he tells the truth, so that you may believe. For these things happened that the Scripture might be fulfilled, "A bone of him will not be broken." Again, another Scripture says, "They will look on him whom they pierced." (John 19:35–37)

> This is the disciple who testifies to these things and who wrote them down. We know that his testimony is true. (John 21:24)

The author stated that he:

1. was a witness of Jesus,
2. wrote down what he saw,
3. observed Jesus fulfilling the Messiah prophecy, and,
4. provided testimony that is the truth.

These are two huge eyewitness statements from an author who "tells the truth, that you may believe" that Jesus was the Jewish Messiah (e.g., Exodus 12:46, Numbers 9:12, Psalm 34:20, and Zachariah 12:10). With five total references to "he" and "his" in those two testimony statements it's obvious that the author wrote his testimony in the third party. But since the name of the author isn't provided, the testimony can't be validated until we determine who he is and positively place him with Jesus.

The author considered eyewitness testimony a crucial component of writing about Jesus because, along with his own statements, he wrote about JB testifying for Jesus (John 1:7, 15, 19, 32, and 34), and Jesus addressing it (John 5:31–38, 8:13–18, and 10:24–25). The author, as one of Jesus' inner circle disciples, took his testimony assignment very seriously. As a starting point, with Peter and Andrew being the two witnesses of Revelation who couldn't write, the author is likely James or John Zebedee, who were Jesus' other two designated eyewitness disciples.

CRLs claim that the Gospel of John was written sometime between 30 and 90 years after Jesus' resurrection. To make matters worse, most scholars conclude that it was written towards the end of that range based on words from a man named Clement of Alexandria. There is no evidence to support the claim that those who lived several generations after Jesus, nor is there evidence to prove the claims of "scholars." Atheists have told me a multitude of times that the Gospels cannot be eyewitness testimony because ALL the scholars say they are passed down stories of tradition written many years after Jesus lived. If they reference specific scholars, I ask them to provide me with one piece of evidence from their favorite scholars to prove their claim, and without exception, they fail to do this, then attack my credentials. The CRL and expert scholar stories don't even make sense because a rational person wonders why the authors would wait so long to document their eyewitness testimony—especially when Jesus commanded them to complete them between 30 and 33 AD.

There is no doubt that the Gospel of John provides personal observational testimony about Jesus because it is packed full of eyewitness details. One prime example is the story of Jesus resurrecting Lazarus from the dead, which describes:

- Who Lazarus was, his family members, and where they all lived.
- Jesus waited to visit Lazarus until there were no doubts that Lazarus had died because he intended to raise Lazarus from the dead.
- Martha met Jesus on the way to their house while Mary stayed at home.
- Situational details about the crowd, the tomb, etc.

Another good example of eyewitness details presented in the Gospel of John is the accounting of two of Jesus' disciples running to the tomb. First, the author described the 'other disciple outran Peter' to the tomb (John 20:4). This completely unnecessary detail indicates the presence and participation by the author. Then, the author captured the event from the perspective of being the unnamed disciple, written as a bystander in the third person:

> [5] Stooping and looking in, he saw the linen cloths lying there; yet he didn't enter in. [6] Then Simon Peter came, following him, and entered into the tomb. He saw the linen cloths lying, [7] and the cloth that had been on his head, not lying with the linen cloths, but rolled up in a place by itself. (John 20:5–7)

The author provided vivid details about what happened when Peter and this other disciple went to Jesus' tomb and found it empty.

The author has not specifically identified the other disciple described here or throughout the Gospel of John because it is "he," "him," or even "his" when something is possessed. Other examples in the Gospel of John of the author being present and writing in the third person include:

- [37] The two disciples heard him speak, and they followed Jesus. . .[40] One of the two who heard John and followed him was Andrew, Simon Peter's brother. (John 1:37–40)
- [23] One of his disciples, whom Jesus loved, was at the table, leaning against Jesus' chest. [24] Simon Peter therefore beckoned to him, and said to him, "Tell us who it is of whom he speaks." [25] He, leaning back, as he was, on Jesus' chest, asked him, "Lord, who is it?" (John 13:23–25)
- Therefore, when Jesus saw his mother and the disciple whom he loved standing there, he said to his mother, "Woman, behold, your son!" (John 19:26)
- That disciple, therefore, whom Jesus loved said to Peter, "It's the Lord!" So when Simon Peter heard that it was the Lord, he wrapped his coat around himself (for he was naked) and threw himself into the sea. (John 21:7)
- Then Peter, turning around, saw a disciple following. This was the disciple whom Jesus loved, the one who had also leaned on Jesus' chest at the supper and asked, "Lord, who is going to betray you?" (John 21:20)

There is no doubt that the eyewitness author who frequently referred to himself as the disciple "whom Jesus loved" is writing his account because he presents numerous extraneous details that indicate he was there to witness them.

The author of the Gospel of John very clearly identified the disciples of Jesus, and through this, we can validate that he was either James or John Zebedee. That author confirmed that there were twelve disciples (John 6:67) but never provided a summary list like the one existing in the Gospel of Mark and copied by Matthew's author:

1. John the Baptist (John 1:15–34, 3:23–26, 5:33)
2. Andrew, one of the two disciples who left John the Baptist to follow Jesus (John 1:40), from Bethsaida (John 1:44)
3. One of Zebedee's brothers (John 21:2), named James or John (Mark 1:19)
4. Another Zebedee brother who witnessed Jesus' resurrection (John 21:2), named John or Mark
5. Andrew's brother, Simon, who Jesus called Peter (John 1:40–42) and was from Bethsaida (John 1:44)
6. Philip (John 1:43, 14:8) from Bethsaida (John 1:44)
7. Nathanael, an honest Israelite (John 1:45–50)
8. Nicodemus, a Pharisee and ruler of the Jews (John 3:1–21, 7:50–51, and 19:39–42)
9. Judas, the son of Simon Iscariot, who would betray Jesus (John 6:71)
10. Thomas (John 11:16, 14:5)
11. Judas, not the son of Iscariot (John 14:22)
12. Joseph of Arimathaea, a secret disciple of Jesus (John 19:38)

All four of the inner circle disciples Jesus assigned to be his eyewitnesses are presented in the Gospel of John, but the two sons of Zebedee are left unnamed. This is an important detail because the Gospel of John is written in the third person, so the author left himself unnamed. There can be no doubt that the author is one of the unnamed Zebedee brothers, John or James.

Mark's author provides an interesting detail about the Zebedee brothers. He stated that Jesus referred to James and John Zebedee as the "Sons of Thunder" (Mark 3:17). The "Sons of Thunder" is capitalized, so it is a formal designation with an important connotation. Jesus' reference to the Zebedee brothers as the "Sons of Thunder" can be explained through the following description of Thunder:

> [27] "Now my soul is troubled. What shall I say? 'Father, save me from this time'? But I came to this time for this cause. [28] Father, glorify your name!" Then a voice came out of the sky, saying, "I have both glorified it and will glorify it again." [29] Therefore, the multitude who stood by and heard it said that it had thundered. Others said, "An angel has spoken to him." (John 12:27–29)

Jesus' full purpose was to come to the earth as a human to present God to the world so that God would be glorified. A multitude of people heard God validate Jesus through the sound of "Thunder." God testified for Jesus through what sounded like "Thunder." James and John weren't God, but they were to provide their testimony for Jesus, and a multitude of people would hear it, read it, and say it is the word of God. God "glorified it [Jesus]" through Thunder and the Zebedee brothers as the "Sons of Thunder" will "glorify it [Jesus] again." Based on this title, both Zebedee brothers wrote their testimony, and since we learn about the Sons of Thunder in the Gospel of Mark, that book, along with the Gospel of John, are likely their testimonies.

The unnamed Zebedee brother who wrote the Gospel of John was very special, as noted through the following that describe him,

- Andrew, the unnamed disciple, and JB became the first to follow Jesus (John 1:37),
- he sat in the honor seat leaning on Jesus' chest (John 13:23),
- a disciple who knew the high priest whom he asked to allow Peter to attend Jesus' trial (John 18:15–16), and,
- he stood at the foot of the cross to hear Jesus assign his mother to him (John 19:25–27)

Both the Zebedee brothers were special, but one was set aside for something even more special.

We have evidence that Jesus treated one disciple very specially because he gave that disciple a vision of the complete future of the NC. We find the important details of that special disciple presented in the documentation of that vision:

> This is the Revelation of Jesus Christ, which God gave him to show to his servants the things which must happen soon, which he sent and made known by his angel to his servant, John, [2] who testified to God's word and of the testimony of Jesus Christ, about everything that he saw. (Revelation 1:1–2)

Note that in that statement, John stated that he has "testified to God's word and of the testimony of Jesus Christ." This is in the past tense, so John has already documented Jesus' words as the word of God prior to Jesus providing him with this vision.

Then, John mentioned himself again by name as the author:

> John, to the seven assemblies that are in Asia: Grace to you and peace from God, who is and who was and who is to come; and from the seven Spirits who are before his throne; (Revelation 1:4)

> I, John, your brother and partner with you in the oppression, Kingdom, and perseverance in Christ Jesus, was on the isle that is called Patmos because of God's Word and the testimony of Jesus Christ. (Revelation 1:9)

> Now I, John, am the one who heard and saw these things. When I heard and saw, I fell down to worship before the feet of the angel who had shown me these things. (Revelation 22:8)

John does not want there to be any doubts that he was the author who has already presented his testimony of Jesus Christ and is presenting more. There is some prevalent theology that John was an old man when he wrote Revelation in Patmos prison. But just as it is for the Gospel names provided by the CRLs, there is no evidence to prove that story of tradition. That story of tradition was created to prevent Andrew and Peter from being considered as the two witnesses of Revelation 11; therefore, the two witnesses prophecy MUST be addressing end-time ART.

Here is some food for thought: What are the chances that John told us four times in Revelation that he was the one who received the vision, but then didn't mention himself or his brother James even once in his testimony about Jesus? A disciple who emphasized testimony throughout his book, wrote two testimony statements confirming he was writing testimony about Jesus, then mentioned himself four times by name in Revelation, is expected to have named himself in his own testimony for Jesus. There is zero chance that he didn't; therefore, we have additional false teacher editing. What are the chances that the Gospels of Matthew and Mark were left unnamed by their authors when they are providing the most important testimony ever to be documented in the world? Again, zero! It makes no sense at all, and the fact that it has happened supports more corruption by the beasts.

Why cause author confusion for eyewitness testimonies of Jesus? Consider that if you have rock-solid testimony of two or three eyewitnesses for Jesus, you don't need the help or interpretations from CRLs to believe. However, if there is a confusing mess mixed in with the words of Paul and others, CRLs need to explain Jesus, and they can create theology that helps them hang on to their jobs and control the word of God. Through uncertainty, CRLs are important and necessary to "help" you understand Jesus and the path to righteousness. If this sounds a bit like the saying, "I'm from the government and I'm here to help you," it is meant to. Through their religion, the ECFs were able to keep control of the word of God.

In summary, based on the eyewitness testimony statements and the evidence presented, there is no doubt that John, one of the special disciples, authored the Gospel of John. He wrote his testimony with his own hand during the decreed 1,290-day timeframe between 30–33 AD. We now have one of the two or three required testimonies to prove Jesus to all people of the world.

JOHN EYEWITNESS JESUS EVIDENCE

1. Jesus is God born as a man with a mission to start the NC (6 BC)
2. Satan attempted to stop the NC from starting (6 BC)
3. Jesus' mission to teach, heal and perform miracles (26–30 AD)
    a. John 1:7, 15, 19, 32, 34, 5:31–38, 8:13–18, and 10:24–25—The author emphasized the importance of eyewitness testimony
    b. John 11:1—12:17 and 20:5–7 provide a few of the numerous situational eyewitness details proving that he was with Jesus and observed his teaching and miracles
    c. John 13:23–25—John was close to Jesus and was in the seat of honor as he leaned "against Jesus' chest" and asked Jesus a question on behalf of Peter
    d. John 21:2—Only two disciples of Jesus are left unnamed, the Zebedee brothers, and the author must be one of them

   e. John 1:37, 13:23, and 19:25–27—The unnamed Zebedee was very special to Jesus

4. Jesus' sacrifice and resurrection (30 AD)
5. Second half of Jesus' seven-year mission (30–33 AD)
   a. John 19:35–37 and John 21:24—John, the disciple of Jesus, testified that he had provided his testimony of Jesus, and he wrote the Gospel of John with his own hand
   b. Revelation 1:1–2, 1:4, 1:9, 22:8—John Zebedee, who received Revelation from Jesus, was special, stated his name, and confirmed his testimony
6. Start of the NC, the Great Tribulation, and the AOD (33 AD)
7. Generation of the Disciples (33–67 AD)
   a. Revelation 1:1–2, 1:4, 1:9, 22:8—John received and documented a vision about the future
8. The NC (33–2333 AD)
9. First half of the NC—the reign of the Beast (33–1333 AD)
10. Second half of Jesus' NC—Jesus' 1000-year reign with his chosen ones (1333–2333 AD)
11. The Time of the End (2333-?)
12. Judgement

14

Searching for Another Witness

Now that I've proven John the disciple to have written the Gospel of John, and Peter and Andrew to be the two witnesses of Revelation, James is the only one of the four eyewitnesses whom Jesus appointed in Mark 13:3 remaining. There are two Gospels left, Matthew and Mark, but there isn't a chance that James copied from another author, so the Gospel of Mark is his only possible documented eyewitness testimony. We know that Jesus appointed James to document his testimony, and we have the Gospel of Mark as the only possible option.

Thus far, the evidence proving James to be the author of the anonymous Gospel of Mark is not overwhelming. James would know that Jesus gave him and his brother the nickname "Sons of Thunder," (Mark 3:17) so that points to James, but this is a long way from the evidence needed. There are a few more personal eyewitness details in the following that indicate James is the author of the Gospel of Mark:

> [19] Going on a little further from there, he saw James, the son of Zebedee, and John, his brother, who were also in the boat mending the nets. [20] Immediately, he called them, and they left their father, Zebedee, in the boat with the hired servants, and went after him. (Mark 1:19–20)

The author is very clear to state that "James is the son of Zebedee" and "John is his brother." If you read the details of this description very carefully, you will realize that the author has stated that James and John are stepbrothers. However, not all English translations capture this detail; about 20% word it differently to remove the author's stepbrother designation. The author of Matthew copied the exact wording, so we know that what was recorded by James carried over (Matthew 4:21). On the flip side, about the same percentage of English translations of Matthew word the comment differently to remove the stepbrother reference. Based on the uncertainty in the translations, this data supports James as the author, but there is an asterisk after it.

But then, on that same account, the author provided additional family details. The author stated that there were "hired servants" in the boat with the Zebedee brothers and that "their father" was with them. These unnecessary details that have nothing to do with Jesus' recruiting James and John indicate that we have read an eyewitness statement of someone who provided their observations. Since it is a description of the Zebedee family and John wrote the Gospel of John, the author MUST be James.

There are other events documented in the Gospel of Mark that, through a process of elimination, prove James was present and was the author. First, the author of Mark recorded an event of Jesus raising a dead girl back to life (Mark 5:35–43). This account of the resurrection of the dead girl is also captured in Matthew 9:23–26, and that version was again copied by that author. The author of Mark provided the eyewitness details of who was present:

> He allowed no one to follow him except Peter, James, and John, the brother of James. (Mark 5:37)

We know that Andrew was present but was edited out of this account by the beast, but this won't change the conclusion. The detail of who went privately with Jesus was not copied over to the account in Matthew, and this is not by accident. The Holy Spirit ensured these details were presented in Mark to tell us that James was present and that one of these eyewitnesses must be the author. By disqualifying the other attendees, John, Peter, and Andrew as authors for the previously mentioned reasons, we know that the Holy Spirit pointed us directly to James as the author of the Gospel of Mark. Likewise, by a process of elimination, James must be the eyewitness and author of another event called the Transfiguration of Jesus (Mark 9:2–13 and Matthew 17:1–13).

There is more evidence that James wrote the Gospel of Mark. The author of the Gospel of Matthew didn't hide the fact that he copied from the author of Mark. Matthew's author copying from Mark's author indicates that the author of Mark was a trusted and valid eyewitness to Jesus. As one of the inner circle disciples who witnessed everything Jesus did, James wrote the perfect testimony to copy from. Furthermore, we know that John had advanced writing skills, and with James growing up in the same household, James likely had the same qualifications.

We know the false teachers DID NOT want evidence left in Mark that would point to James as the author, so they picked it clean. But even so, we have already presented a fair number of data points indicating that James is the author of that Gospel. But through evaluating the next event of Jesus' healing, Peter's mother-in-law found in Matthew 8:14–15 and Mark 1:29–31, we get solid confirmation of James as the author of the Gospel of Mark:

1. JESUS ENTERS THE HOUSE

> Matthew 8:14
> When Jesus came into Peter's house, he saw his wife's mother lying sick with a fever.
>
> Mark 1:29–30
> Immediately, when they had come out of the synagogue, they came into the house of Simon and Andrew, with James and John. Now Simon's wife's mother lay sick with a fever, and immediately they told him about her.

Analysis: Mark's author told us who was present and that the house they were in wasn't only Simon's house, it was Simon's AND Andrew's house. Mark's author also told us what was happening leading up to this event, then what happened when they arrived. Matthew's author presented none of these details, so again, Matthew's author is proven to have copied the account from Mark's author. Mark's author presented eyewitness details, so he was one of the four who were present. By default, it must be James' testimony because John is the author of the Gospel of John, and Simon and Andrew were the two witnesses who couldn't write.

In addition, Mark's author referred to Peter as Simon (Mark 1:30), and this proves James to be the author. Only John, Peter, and Andrew spent time with Jesus to hear Jesus change Simon's name to Peter on that first day (John 1:39–42). Per the author of Mark, James first observed Jesus with the disciples when Jesus walked by the shore to recruit Simon and Andrew in a boat (Mark 1:16–18), then he recruited James and John in another boat (Mark 1:19–20). Afterwards, these four disciples went to the synagogue (Mark 1:21–28), then left to immediately go to the house of Simon and Andrew, where Jesus healed

Simon's mother-in-law (Mark 1:29–31). James is the only one of the four who went to that house who didn't know Jesus had changed Simon's name to Peter; therefore, referring to Peter as Simon in Mark 1:30 indicates the event description came from James. James continued to refer to Peter as Simon until Mark 3:16, after which all eighteen references were to "Peter." Once James found out that Jesus changed Simon's name to Peter, he consistently used that designation.

2. JESUS HEALS THE WOMAN

> Matthew 8:15
> He touched her hand, and the fever left her. So she got up and served him.

> Mark 1:31
> He came and took her by the hand and raised her up. The fever left her immediately, and she served them.

Analysis: Mark's author again provides additional eyewitness details not included in Matthew—Jesus "went to her," then "took her by the hand" and "raised her up." Mark's author was James, one of the four disciples who was present. Matthew's author wasn't there and copied from James because James was a trusted eyewitness.

Finally, there is one additional event that has evidence buried in the details that also confirms James to be the author of the Gospel of Mark. The Zebedee brothers requested Jesus to grant them the seats of honor next to him (Mark 10:35–41 and Matthew 20:20–24). Mark's author confirmed that the two brothers were alone with Jesus:

> When the ten heard it, they began to be indignant toward James and John. (Mark 10:41)

The only ones present with Jesus who could testify to this event were James and John, because the other ten disciples were not there to witness it. Since ONLY James and John were present to witness this exchange with Jesus, one of the two MUST be the author. John wrote his own account and didn't mention this event, so the author wasn't John and had to be James.

The version in Mark is a slam dunk for finding out that James is the author of the Gospel of Mark, but the beasts couldn't allow this. The beasts wanted everyone to believe that the Gospel written by James was the words of Peter, documented by John Mark. The false teachers had two options: remove Mark 10:35–41 or make a slight edit to the version in Matthew to remove the slam dunk proving James as the author. They chose the edit by adding another attendee to that event—James' and John's mother:

> [20] Then the mother of the sons of Zebedee came to him with her sons, kneeling and asking a certain thing of him. [21] He said to her, "What do you want?" She said to him, "Command that these, my two sons, may sit, one on your right hand and one on your left hand, in your Kingdom." (Matthew 20:20–21)

> [35] James and John, the sons of Zebedee, came near to him, saying, "Teacher, we want you to do for us whatever we will ask." [36] He said to them, "What do you want me to do for you? [37] They said to him, "Grant to us that we may sit, one at your right hand and one at your left hand, in your glory." (Mark 10:35–37)

In Matthew, there are no longer only two people with Jesus because Zebedee's brother's mother is with them. With that one very important detail, the slam dunk that James had been the author of the event went away because there is now confusion in the story to focus on, rather than considering where this account came from.

Except for that major edit in Matthew, the situational details are duplicated in that copied account. However, when the false teachers edited that account to add Zebedee's mother, they slipped up and forgot to change a very important detail that reveals their editing:

> But Jesus answered, "You don't know what you are asking. Are you able to drink the cup that I am about to drink, and be baptized with the baptism that I am baptized with?" They said to him, "We are able." (Matthew 20:22)

> [38] But Jesus said to them, "You don't know what you are asking. Are you able to drink the cup that I drink, and to be baptized with the baptism that I am baptized with?" [39] They said to him, "We are able." (Mark 10:38–39)

They didn't edit Jesus' response to indicate that their mother had asked the question rather than the brothers. If their mother had asked the question as written in Matthew, Jesus' response would be to their mother, it wouldn't be "YOU don't know what YOU are asking. Are YOU able to drink the cup. . ." The beast forgot to change Jesus' response to indicate that Zebedee's mother was there asking the question. In summary, with the confusion eliminated, we can focus on who was present—only James and John, and this proves James as the author.

As a side note, the Zebedee brothers had requested that Jesus (Mark 10:37), "Grant to us that we may sit, one at your right hand and one at your left hand, in your glory." Jesus responded by telling the brothers, "But to sit at my right hand and at my left hand is not mine to give, but for whom it has been prepared." But God likely had the seats prepared for the two brothers because John told us twice that he was in the honor seat next to Jesus (John 13:25 and 21:20). Then there is the evidence proving the brothers drank from the same cup Jesus did. We know that James was executed for following Jesus (Acts 12:2), but we also know that Andrew and Peter were executed as the two witnesses. We know that Peter wasn't in the other seat next to Jesus because he had to ask John to ask Jesus a question. Although we aren't told who was in the other seat of honor at the last supper, the documentation indicates it to be James or Andrew, who drank from the same cup as Jesus.

In summary, false teachers who took the NT for themselves proclaimed that John Mark wrote the Gospel of Mark by writing down the words of Peter. The false teachers couldn't claim Peter to be the leader of the NC without a written testimony. Their claim, without any evidence to support it, was nonsensical. Through analysis, I have proven that James is, beyond a doubt, the author of the Gospel of Mark. Considering that the beast hid James to promote John Mark as the author, finding these details that James wrote the Gospel of Mark is spite of the fraud, is incredible. Through the work of the Holy Spirit, God ensured every detail in the Gospels was documented just right—just as Jesus promised (John 14:26), otherwise these details wouldn't exist.

The world now has two proven eyewitness testimonies of Jesus from the Sons of Thunder, the Zebedee brothers named James and John. Praise God because we have now met Deuteronomy 17:6 and 19:15 eyewitness requirements to prove Jesus existed. I still have one more Gospel to examine. Then, to wrap up the investigation, I will need to prove Jesus performed miracles, died on the cross, and resurrected himself from the dead. But we are off to a great start!

JAMES EYEWITNESS JESUS EVIDENCE

1. Jesus is God born as a man with a mission to start the NC (6 BC)
2. Satan attempted to stop the NC from starting (6 BC)
3. Jesus' mission to teach, heal and perform miracles (26–30 AD)
   a. John 12:27–29, Mark 3:17—Jesus named John and James Zebedee the Sons of Thunder to reveal them both as writing the testimony that validates Jesus as God
   b. Mark 13:3—With Andrew and Peter being unable to write and chosen as the two witnesses of Revelation 11, and John having documented the Gospel of John, James must be the author of the Gospel of Mark
   c. Mark 1:19–20—The author of Mark provided Zebedee household eyewitness details that would come from one of the Zebedee brothers
   d. Mark 1:29–31—One of numerous events copied by Matthew's author, indicating that the author of Mark is a trusted eyewitness of Jesus
   e. Mark 1:19–20, 29–31, 5:37, 9:2—James, who was present with the other inner circle disciples is proven to have authored the Gospel of Mark
   f. Mark 1:30, 3:16—The author referred to Peter as Simon in Mark 1:30 because he hadn't heard Jesus' change Simon's name to Peter until Mark 3:16
   g. Mark 10:35–41—The Zebedee brothers were the only ones present; therefore, the eyewitness testimony had to come from James
4. Jesus' sacrifice and resurrection (30 AD)
5. Second half of Jesus' seven-year mission (30–33 AD)
   a. James wrote his testimony in a book now referred to as the Gospel of Mark
6. Start of the NC, the Great Tribulation, and the AOD (33 AD)
7. Generation of the Disciples (33–67 AD)
   a. Acts 12:2—James was executed for his faith and testimony of Jesus
8. The NC (33–2333 AD)

9. First half of the NC—the reign of the Beast (33–1333 AD)
    a. ECFs eliminated James as the author of an eyewitness testimony referred to now as the Gospel of Mark, and stated that John Mark wrote down Peter's words in it
10. Second half of Jesus' NC—Jesus' 1000-year reign with his chosen ones (1333–2333 AD)
11. The Time of the End (2333-?)
12. Judgement

15

The Search for Matthew's 'Real' Author

But why stop with two proven eyewitness testimonies when there is another Gospel with an author who copied from James, who is a proven eyewitness? Some may think that the fact that Matthew's author copied James' events is a bad thing, but it is not. The author of Matthew could have created stories of Jesus or copied from somebody who wasn't a trusted eyewitness, but he didn't—he chose a trusted eyewitness chosen by Jesus to provide his testimony. The only reason for Matthew's author to copy a bunch of information into his testimony to prove the story of Jesus to be true is that he didn't witness all the information he needed. I know that last statement to be true only because Matthew's author presented an ample amount of independent documentation with numerous examples of eyewitness details.

The author provided crucial and unique details of the trial of Jesus. We know that Pilate confided in the author because the author knew what Pilate thought: "For he [Pilate] knew that because of envy they had delivered him [Jesus] up" (Matthew 27:18). He also knew that Pilate received a private message from his wife during the trial:

> While he [Pilate] was sitting on the judgment seat, his wife sent to him, saying, "Have nothing to do with that righteous man, for I have suffered many things today in a dream because of him." (Matthew 27:19)

I've received and observed others receiving private messages like this during important negotiations and meetings. In most cases, the message content is kept private, and only a few select individuals are made aware of the message contents. The fact that the content of this personal message received in the middle of an ongoing hectic trial was only recorded by this author indicates he was close to Pilate.

The author presented another interesting detail:

> So when Pilate saw that nothing was being gained, but rather that a disturbance was starting, he took water and washed his hands before the multitude, saying, "I am innocent of the blood of his righteous person. You see to it." All the people answered, "May his blood be on us and on our children!" (Matthew 27:24–25)

The author reported that Pilate washed his hands and stated that although the governor was allowing Jesus to be executed, he claimed he was not to be held responsible. The author saw Pilate's public display for objecting to the execution of Jesus and noted the crowd's reaction.

There is ample information validating the author as a religious leader who was present to record the following independent information:

- Religious leader's interaction with Judas the traitor:
    - After Jesus was condemned, the chief priests AND elders observed Judas' remorse for turning in Jesus and witnessed Judas return the 30 pieces of silver (Matthew 27:3–4)
    - The author reported that Judas left and hanged himself (Matthew 27:5)
    - The chief priests met and agreed to take the money, and since the law did not permit the money to be put into the treasury, they bought a field as a burial place for strangers (Matthew 27:6–7)
- Then there are the details of the guards that only a religious leader who knew Pilate and was with the religious leaders who wanted Jesus' tomb secured would know and report (Matthew 27:62—28:15). He heard some of the following eyewitness details from the tomb guarding event:
    - The day after the preparation day, the chief priests and Pharisees met with Governor Pilate to get the tomb guarded (Matthew 27:62)
    - The religious leaders heard Jesus claim that he would rise from the dead after three days, necessitating the tomb guards (Matthew 27:63–64)
    - Pilate assigned them a guard (Matthew 27:65)

- o The scribes and Pharisees went with the guard and secured the tomb by sealing the stone (Matthew 27:66)

Early in the Gospel of Matthew, the independently provided material is consistent with the interests of a Jewish religious leader with connections to Jesus' family, other religious leaders, and the Roman rulers. First, the author provided the genealogy of Jesus, connecting him to the line of King David (Matthew 1:1–17). Next, the author provided details of the conception, birth, and early years of Jesus—likely obtained from the author's interaction with the following sources:

- Mary and/or Joseph, the parents of Jesus (Matthew 1:18–25, 2:13–15 and 19–23)
- The Wise Men, which is a term referring to teachers, scientists, physicians, astrologers, seers, interpreters of dreams, or sorcerers (Matthew 2:1–2 and 7–12)
- King Herod (2:3–4, 7–8 and 16–17)
- Chief Priests and Scribes (2:5–6)

The author was schooled in scripture because in the first two chapters of Matthew, there are references to events in Jesus' life that fulfilled Messianic prophecy. Matthew's author obtained this opening information from a variety of sources that only a religious leader who was in the service of King Herod would have been able to obtain and document.

An important clue obtained from this early information is that we get an idea of the age of the author. Since this author is an established religious leader who interacted with the governing rulers at the time of Jesus' birth about 6 BC, he was an older man by the time Jesus' mission started over thirty years later in 26 AD. That's an important and interesting clue because John documented Jesus teaching a religious leader who claimed to be an old man when he met Jesus:

> Now there was a man of the Pharisees named Nicodemus, a ruler of the Jews. [2] He came to Jesus by night and said to him, "Rabbi, we know that you are a teacher come from God, for no one can do these signs that you do, unless God is with him." [3] Jesus answered him, "Most certainly I tell you, unless one is born anew, he can't see God's Kingdom." [4] Nicodemus said to him, "How can a man be born when he is old? Can he enter a second time into his mother's womb and be born?" (John 3:1–4)

From the documentation, we know that Nicodemus had already somewhat investigated Jesus because he stated Jesus was a teacher who had "come from God." Claiming that Jesus came from God meant this religious leader had already concluded that Jesus was at a minimum a prophet. His claim was a powerful and unpopular statement coming from a Pharisee and ruler of the Jews because there are numerous examples in the Gospels of how badly the religious elite detested Jesus. Nicodemus had to meet Jesus under the cover of darkness. At that introduction meeting with Jesus, Nicodemus asked him, "How can a man be born when he is old?" This indicates that Nicodemus was an old man when he finally met Jesus, and this connects him to the early chapters in Matthew. It's easy to see how Nicodemus is the perfect fit to be the author of the Gospel of Matthew.

As I documented earlier, John considered Nicodemus to be a disciple of Jesus—albeit a secret one. As a ruler of the Jews, Nicodemus certainly would have had connections to the Government leaders. When King Herod summoned the "Chief priests and scribes of the people," Nicodemus would have been with them, so he recorded what he witnessed. Nicodemus would have either been with King Herod when the King commanded the Wise Men to search for Jesus, or he would have documented testimony from those who were present. In addition, a Jewish religious leader certainly would have been interested in the scuttlebutt about Jesus fulfilling the prophecy of the Jewish Messiah that was spreading like wildfire. As a religious leader, Nicodemus would have had access to testimony from Jesus' family about the details surrounding Jesus' birth and his early years.

Nicodemus had done his homework prior to meeting Jesus. The sermon on the mount is recorded only by Matthew's author (Matthew 5:1—7:29), proving that Nicodemus was in the audience listening to Jesus. Everything in that sermon is of interest to a religious leader and ruler of the Jews.

The Holy Spirit knew the actions of the false teachers to hide Nicodemus from the world, so he had John document Nicodemus immediately after John stated the importance of having eyewitness testimony of Jesus resurrected (John 2:22—3:21). Nicodemus got top billing in the Gospel of John because he was to have that very important testimonial role and the Holy Spirit wanted you to know that. Consider that the most famous and commonly recited verse in all of scripture, John 3:16, was spoken by Jesus to Nicodemus.

John also documented that Nicodemus stood up for Jesus when a group of religious leaders had referred to Jesus as a false prophet:

> [50] Nicodemus (he who came to him by night, being one of them) said to them, [51] "Does our law judge a man unless it first hears from him personally and knows what he does?" They answered him, "Are you also from Galilee? Search and see that no prophet has arisen out of Galilee." (John 7:50–52)

Nicodemus challenged the religious leaders who judged Jesus without hearing from him themselves. What happened next provides undisputed proof that Nicodemus was the author of the Gospel of Matthew. After Nicodemus was challenged to "Search and see that no prophet has arisen out of Galilee," John recorded what happened next:

> [53] Everyone went to his own house, [1] but Jesus went to the Mount of Olives. (John 7:53—8:1)

Don't be fooled by these two verses because that isn't what John wrote. In the footnotes, the World English Bible states that textual critics have lower confidence that John 7:53—8:11 is original. The New International Version study Bible, Published by Zondervan © 2011, page 1781, claims, "The earliest manuscripts and many other ancient witnesses do not have John 7:53—8:11." In summary, what John wrote next is MISSING because it would have proven Nicodemus as the author of the Gospel of Matthew.

There's more about Nicodemus written in John's Gospel. Nicodemus went with another secret disciple of Jesus named Joseph to obtain Jesus' body and entomb it:

> [38] After these things, Joseph of Arimathea, being a disciple of Jesus, but secretly for fear of the Jews, asked Pilate that he might take away Jesus' body. Pilate gave him permission. He came therefore and took away his body. [39] Nicodemus, who at first came to Jesus by night, also came bringing a mixture of myrrh and aloes, about a hundred Roman pounds. (John 19:38–39)

The account is written vaguely so that it doesn't specifically name Nicodemus requesting the body of Jesus from Pilate, but it was written that way to escape the false teacher editing. We know that Nicodemus, as a ruler of the Jews, had access to Pilate. Based on his connection to the King and since both Joseph and Nicodemus were secret disciples of Jesus, it's not a stretch to believe that Nicodemus was with Joseph when they went to see Pilate to ask him to release Jesus' body to them.

There is one additional very important event that proves Nicodemus as the author. There is a resurrection event that has been tampered with by the false teachers that was written by him, but he doesn't get credit for it, and it isn't even presented in the Gospel of Matthew. Through extensive analysis later, I will provide the evidence that Nicodemus was commissioned by Jesus to be an eyewitness, and that, as expected, he documented the resurrection of Jesus. Nicodemus would not have written a testimony for Jesus had he not witnessed Jesus resurrected, and as you will see, the resurrection accounts in Matthew are not eyewitness testimony; they are fictional false teacher editing. Jesus planned for his complete story to be told through eyewitness testimony, so we can be assured that there is much more to the story of Nicodemus that has been removed from the Gospels—including John 7:53—8:11.

Without a doubt, the author of the Gospel of Matthew is Nicodemus, a religious leader and Jewish ruler who knew the disciples, was a close friend of John's, and was also friends with James, whom he copied from. Nicodemus was a disciple of Jesus, albeit a secret one. John was guided by the Holy Spirit to provide all the details of Nicodemus so that Nicodemus' identity as the author of the Gospel of Matthew would be revealed. Nicodemus was a dedicated and sincere follower of Jesus, and John's inclusion of him as one of the twelve disciples was certainly justified. As a religious leader with proven access to Jesus and his disciples, Nicodemus had the religious background and skills to perform a thorough and complete investigation of Jesus.

The complete story of Jesus cannot be told without the details provided to us by a ruler of the Jews who would witness Judas throwing the coins, Pilate's actions and reactions, the guards, and the contempt for Jesus the other Jewish leaders had. Jesus had a plan for Nicodemus to provide his complete testimony to be written and presented to the world, but false teachers had other plans, and they eliminated Nicodemus as an author just as they eliminated Andrew from being one of Jesus' inner circle disciples. The false teachers needed Matthew, not Nicodemus.

NICODEMUS EYEWITNESS JESUS EVIDENCE

1. Jesus is God born as a man with a mission to start the NC (6 BC)
2. Satan attempted to stop the NC from starting (6 BC)

3. Jesus' mission to teach, heal and perform miracles (26–30 AD)
    a. John 3:1–21, 7:50–51, 19:39–42—Nicodemus was being taught and connected to Jesus
    b. Matthew 5:1—7:29—Nicodemus sat in the audience to hear Jesus' sermon that addressed subjects of interest to a religious leader
    c. John 7:53—8:11—Removed and replaced to hide Nicodemus from being recognized by his response to a Pharisee challenge to investigate Jesus as the Messiah
    d. Matthew 27:1–66—Numerous eyewitness details of religious leader interaction with Judas the traitor, Jesus' interrogators, the tomb guards
4. Jesus' sacrifice and resurrection (30 AD)
5. Second half of Jesus' seven-year mission (30–33 AD)
    a. Nicodemus, an old man who was a secret disciple of Jesus, documented his testimony in a book that is now referred to as the Gospel of Matthew
6. Start of the NC, the Great Tribulation, and the AOD (33 AD)
7. Generation of the Disciples (33–67 AD)
8. The NC (33–2333 AD)
9. First half of the NC—the reign of the Beast (33–1333 AD)
    a. ECFs eliminated Nicodemus as the author of an eyewitness testimony and renamed it after a disciple named Matthew, whom they created to observe events they edited
10. Second half of Jesus' NC—Jesus' 1000-year reign with his chosen ones (1333–2333 AD)
11. The Time of the End (2333-?)
12. Judgement

16

Why Matthew Instead of Nicodemus?

THROUGH THE BEASTS, JAMES became John Mark, also called Mark, who wrote the words of Peter, and Nicodemus became a created disciple named Matthew. Two eyewitnesses who provided their testimony about Jesus ceased to exist through the beast corruption of the NC. It's easy to understand why the beast needed John Mark instead of James. Without John Mark writing the words of Peter, the leader of the Catholic Church would not have written his testimony of Jesus, and this was unacceptable. It didn't hurt for the beast to claim that John Mark's words, taken from Peter, were copied by the other authors because the disciples revered Peter.

Determining the reason for false teachers to have created a disciple named Matthew, then attributing Nicodemus' Gospel to him, is not as obvious—until we dig into the details. First, the Gospel that Nicodemus wrote was the perfect document to rename and attribute the testimony to another. Nicodemus did not witness most of the miracles of Jesus, so he copied that testimony from James to make his testimony complete. With some edits and rearrangement of the copied event descriptions, Nicodemus' testimony was easily presented as the eyewitness testimony from another disciple of Jesus, a created one named Matthew.

The Gospel of Nicodemus was changed to the Gospel of Matthew, and Matthew became one of the twelve who witnessed Jesus' teaching, healing, and performing miracles. This was extremely important for the beast because they were to make crucial edits that would provide the foundation for their new NC organization, which they referred to as the Catholic Church. Matthew was needed to witness Peter walking on water like Jesus, and observe and document Jesus' assigning Peter to lead the NC. These two edits to the Gospel of Matthew made the beast coup possible because, through them, Peter became a disciple whom Jesus appointed to lead the NC, AND he became the only disciple who was to perform a miracle side by side with Jesus.

I'll closely examine both these events. First up is the analysis of the event describing a discussion between Jesus and his disciples, starting with a question (Matthew 16:13–20 and Mark 8:27–30).

1. JESUS ASKS THE DISCIPLES A QUESTION

> Matthew 16:13
> Now when Jesus came into the parts of Caesarea Philippi, he asked his disciples, saying, "Who do men say that I, the Son of Man, am?"
>
> Mark 8:27
> Jesus went out, with his disciples, into the villages of Caesarea Philippi. On the way, he asked his disciples, "Who do men say that I am?"

Analysis: The details in these two verses, who was present, what was said, and the location where it took place are all the same, proving that Matthew's author Nicodemus copied this event from James. The copied account in Matthew has been slightly reworded and rearranged to make it appear as though the created author Matthew, observed the same event that James [Mark] did, but provided slightly different details.

2. JESUS RECEIVED AN ANSWER FROM THE DISCIPLES

> Matthew 16:14
> They said, "Some say John the Baptizer, some, Elijah, and others, Jeremiah or one of the prophets."
>
> Mark 8:28
> They told him, "John the Baptizer, and others say Elijah, but others, one of the prophets."

Analysis: These two accounts are once again identical except for some rearrangement and another addition to the words attributed to Jesus in Matthew. Again, the slight change to the words of Jesus is an obvious edit that helps to make it appear as though a disciple named Matthew is also present but has witnessed the words of Jesus a bit differently.

3. JESUS WANTS TO KNOW WHAT THE DISCIPLES THINK

> Matthew 16:15–16
> He said to them, "But who do you say that I am?" Simon Peter answered, "You are the Christ, the Son of the living God."
>
> Mark 8:29
> He said to them, "But who do you say that I am?" Peter answered, "You are the Christ."

Analysis: This is the third time in this event that there is obvious duplication between the two accounts, with slight edits to the spoken words of Jesus by two eyewitnesses. But this time the false teachers slipped up. James in Mark wrote "Peter," and the edited account has changed that reference to "Simon Peter." John referred to Peter as "Simon Peter" fifteen times in his Gospel, but neither James nor Nicodemus [Matthew] used this term even once. The term "Simon Peter" is an unexpected outlier signaling a beast edit, just as there was that slip-up in terminology, identifying James as the author of Mark when Jesus healed Peter's mother-in-law. The false teachers also added the words "the Son of the living God" to Peter's response, and as you will find in the next section, this term also reveals fraud through editing.

4. JESUS REWARDS PETER

> Matthew 16:17–19
> 17 Jesus answered him, "Blessed are you, Simon Bar Jonah, for flesh and blood has not revealed this to you, but my Father who is in heaven. 18 I also tell you that you are Peter, and on this rock I will build my assembly, and the gates of Hades will not prevail against it. 19 I will give to you the keys of the Kingdom of Heaven, and whatever you bind on earth will have been bound in heaven; and whatever you release on earth will have been released in heaven."

Analysis: This section is without a doubt an edit to a copied version, because it isn't documented in the original. These very important and highly debated verses create the foundation for the Catholic Church, as I presented earlier

(Catechism #880). James [Mark] didn't witness Jesus rewarding Peter, and neither did Nicodemus [Matthew].

Jesus even warned us in advance to reject this edited copy that has Jesus rewarding Peter for telling Jesus he is "the Christ, the Son of the living God." John recorded Peter telling Jesus the same exact thing, but instead of Jesus rewarding Peter for that, Jesus warned about deceit:

> [68] *Simon Peter answered him, "Lord, to whom would we go? You have the words of eternal life.* [69] *We have come to believe and know that you are the Christ, the Son of the living God." (John 6:68–69)*

Notice Jesus' response:

> *Jesus answered them, "Didn't I choose you, the twelve, and one of you is a devil?"* [71] *Now he spoke of Judas, the son of Simon Iscariot, for it was he who would betray him, being one of the twelve. (John 6:70–71)*

Jesus followed up that comment by Peter with a warning about a traitor. Through this completely opposite reaction of Jesus to the same comment by Peter, I believe that the Holy Spirit left breadcrumbs leading to a warning about Matthew 16:17–19 that those same words would be used to deceive.

It is common knowledge that without Matthew 16:17–19, the Catholic Church does not exist. The Catholics claimed in Catechism #880 that Jesus placed Peter "at the head" of the Church and the Catholic pope is "Peter's successor." The references for that claim about Peter in #880 are [398] and [399] which takes readers to LG 19, then that document references (146)(3) which will finally take readers to Matthew 16:18. The Catholic Church does not like to admit their foundation reliance on that one verse in Matthew, so it took a bit of pulling on the reference string to get to the truth.*

5. AN UNUSUAL ENDING

> Matthew 16:20
> Then he commanded the disciples that they should tell no one that he was Jesus the Christ.
>
> Mark 8:30
> He commanded them that they should tell no one about him.

Analysis: Again, there is duplication of the accounts with a few words added to Matthew to make it appear as though Matthew 16:17–19 is just another observation by that author. But did Jesus really command the disciples to be silent about Jesus being "the Christ?" From the Gospels, we know that:

- *The first thing Andrew did when he met Jesus was to go find Peter to tell him he had found the Christ (John 1:41). Peter was told from day one that Jesus was the Messiah.*
- *Jesus confirmed he was the Messiah to an unnamed woman at a well, and,*
- *Jesus also told religious leaders that he was the Messiah.*

Jesus as the Messiah was not to be a secret—it was shared among the disciples, the public, and with religious leaders. I believe that James heard this comment by Jesus, and Nicodemus copied it because Jesus wanted future generations to look at this section of his words and question what was written. Jesus knew in advance that the beasts would use this event to take control of the NC. Therefore, Jesus' comment to be silent, just like Jesus' other response to Peter's words, were meant to get your attention that something isn't right, so read and consider the contents carefully.

But even with all the edits thus far, including Matthew 16:17–19, the beasts still wanted more evidence, and there isn't anything better than having Peter perform a miracle with Jesus. There are three accounts of Jesus walking on water (Matthew 14:22–32, Mark 6:45–52, and John 6:16–26), but only one of them includes a description of Peter walking on the water with Jesus. I'll bet by now you know which one of the three is the Gospel that presents it.

1. THE DISCIPLES LEAVE JESUS AND TAKE A BOAT RIDE

> Matthew 14:22–24
> 22 Immediately, Jesus made the disciples get into the boat and go ahead of him to the other side, while he sent the multitudes away. 23 After he had sent the multitudes away, he went up into the mountain by himself to pray. When evening had come, he was there alone. 24 But the boat was now in the middle of the sea,

> Mark 6:45–47
> 45 Immediately he made his disciples get into the boat, and go ahead to the other side, to Bethsaida, while he himself sent the multitude away. 46 After he had taken leave of them, he went up the

mountain to pray. [47] When evening had come, the boat was in the middle of the sea, and he was alone on the land.

John 6:15–17
[15] Jesus therefore, perceiving that they were about to come and take him by force to make him king, withdrew again to the mountain by himself. [16] When evening came, his disciples went down to the sea. [17] They entered into the boat, and were going over the sea to Capernaum.

Analysis: The version in Matthew is a reworded and rearranged duplicate of what James wrote in Mark. The eyewitness details, except for the Bethsaida destination presented by James, were copied by Matthew's author, Nicodemus, who was not in the boat. The accounts from eyewitnesses James and John differ slightly, as expected. James stated Bethsaida was the destination, Jesus sent the crowd away, and that Jesus went up the mountain to pray. John provided a different destination named Capernaum that was in the same direction and vicinity as Bethsaida. John didn't state that Jesus sent the crowd away; he had a different observation. John reported that Jesus knew the crowd was about to take him by force, so he withdrew to the mountain. John doesn't mention Jesus' praying. The separate specific eyewitness details prove that what's written in Mark and John is from documented observations of the same event.

2. THE DISCIPLES FACE ADVERSITY

Matthew 14:24
[24] distressed by the waves, for the wind was contrary.

Mark 6:48
[48] Seeing them distressed in rowing, for the wind was contrary to them,

John 6:17–18
[17] It was now dark, and Jesus had not come to them. [18] The sea was tossed by a great wind blowing.

Analysis: Again, Nicodemus has copied from James, and the parts have been slightly edited to make it appear as though Matthew was present to witness this event. John tells us the disciples had waited for Jesus, but he didn't show up. John also observed that not only was the wind just "contrary," it was a "great wind blowing" that was making waves.

3. JESUS WALKS ON WATER AND THE DISCIPLES REACT

Matthew 14:25–26
[25] In the fourth watch of the night, Jesus came to them, walking on the sea. [26] When the disciples saw him walking on the sea, they were troubled, saying, "It's a ghost!" and they cried out for fear.

Mark 6:48–50
[48] about the fourth watch of the night he came to them, walking
on the sea, and he would have passed by them, [49] but they, when
they saw him walking on the sea, supposed that it was a ghost, and
cried out; [50] for they all saw him, and were troubled.

John 6:19
[19] When therefore they had rowed about twenty-five or thirty stadia, they saw Jesus walking on the sea, and drawing near to the boat; and they were afraid.

Analysis: The version in Matthew is again a rearranged copy of what James recorded, except that James recorded his personal reaction to observing Jesus, and Nicodemus didn't copy that. James was concerned that Jesus was going to continue walking on the water past the disciples in the boat; he did not have the confidence that Jesus was there for them. John's reaction was a bit different. Although like the other disciples, John was afraid, he considered Jesus to be heading towards the boat. John added details to describe where they were on the lake—about 2-1/2 to 3 miles, and as James noted earlier, in the middle of the lake. Again, there is evidence that James and John are present and are providing the details of what they observed.

4. JESUS' RESPONSE

Matthew 14:27
[27] But immediately Jesus spoke to them, saying, "Cheer up! It is I! Don't be afraid."

Mark 6:50
[50] But he immediately spoke with them, and said to them, "Cheer up! It is I! Don't be afraid."

John 6:20–21
[20] But he said to them, "It is I. Don't be afraid."

Analysis: John didn't hear Jesus tell the disciples to cheer up, because Jesus said that directly to James. The disciples were afraid when they saw Jesus walking on the water, but James was panicking—he was a Jesus skeptic and possibly even a sourpuss who was worried that Jesus was going to walk past the boat and he would drown. Jesus told James to "Cheer up!" because James needed encouragement.

5. PETER WALKS ON WATER

Matthew 14:28–31
[28] Peter answered him and said, "Lord, if it is you, command me
to come to you on the waters." [29] He said, "Come!" Peter stepped
down from the boat and walked on the water to come to Jesus.
[30] But when he saw that the wind was strong, he was afraid, and
beginning to sink, he cried out, saying, "Lord, save me!" [31] Immediately, Jesus stretched out his hand, took hold of him, and said
to him, "You of little faith, why did you doubt?"

Analysis: James and John, the two authors who were in the boat, didn't record Peter's exchange with Jesus, nor did they observe Peter walking on the water. Without a doubt, Nicodemus has copied this event from James, and it has been edited by false teachers to make it appear as though Peter was observed walking on water with Jesus.

6. JESUS ENTERED THE BOAT

Matthew 14:32
[32] When they got up into the boat, the wind ceased.

Mark 6:51
[51] He got into the boat with them; and the wind ceased, and they were very amazed among themselves, and marveled;

John 6:21
[21] They were willing therefore to receive him into the boat. Immediately the boat was at the land where they were going.

Analysis: Nicodemus copied this observation from James but left off the reaction the disciples had to the event to prove that he wasn't there to witness it. I hope you have noticed that Nicodemus is copying the details of the event but leaving off the reactions. John recorded that the disciples "were willing" to let Jesus get into the boat, and that's a very interesting comment that may explain Jesus telling James to "Cheer up!" Think about that comment—Jesus just walked on water, and his disciples in the boat were "willing" to let him board. About 75% of the English translations confirm that the disciples were "willing to let Jesus enter the boat." There is no possible scenario that has the disciples rejecting Jesus from boarding the boat; therefore, there is more to that comment. My understanding of this is that the disciples were having fun with Jesus.

Visualize the disciples' reaction to Jesus' walking on the water while somewhat timidly stating, 'Yah Jesus, you have shown us a lot of miraculous things, and now you even prove that you can walk on the water!' This would explain Jesus telling James to lighten up. The disciples were in a lighthearted mood, but James was taking what happened too seriously. We get a bit of insight into James' personality. He is a bit of a loner because John didn't have him with the disciples when they first met Jesus, nor did John run and get James like Andrew ran to get his brother. James also didn't go with John and Jesus to witness Lazarus' resurrection (you can determine from analyzing Jesus' anointing event descriptions in Mark 14:3–9 and John 12:1–11 that prove James didn't know Lazarus and his family). James was the Zebedee who took things too seriously.

In summary, James didn't report Jesus rewarding Peter with the keys to the NC for proclaiming Jesus to be the Son of the Living God. In addition, James and John didn't record Peter walking on the water because it didn't happen. Both are stories created by false teachers to seal the deal for Peter to be like Jesus and have his name forever be used by the beasts to claim the NC for themselves. Therefore, with the clear motive of the beasts to take control of the NC through Peter, Matthew 16:17–19 and 8:29–31 support that motive, and additional ECF fraud through proven Gospel editing has been revealed.

I can't overemphasize the importance of those two edits. Without these two edits, the Catholic Church does not exist. The most powerful entity that ever existed in the history of the world—the Catholic Church, built its foundation on those two edicts, then supported their claim to the NC of Jesus with its following additional fraudulent actions:

- Replaced James as the author of the Gospel of Mark with a man named John Mark, who was stated to have written Peter's words so that Peter had documented Jesus' testimony

- Edited Andrew out of the inner circle of Jesus and most Gospel documentation to eliminate Peter's brother as a competition for Peter
- Created a disciple named Matthew through:
    - o editing a copied version of the tax collector story (Matthew 9:9–11)
    - o creating lists of the twelve disciples that included Matthew in the lists and inserted them into both Matthew and Mark (Matthew 10:2–4 and Mark 3:14–19)
    - o specifically noted that Matthew was the tax collector in the list of the twelve disciples copied into Matthew
    - o strategically edited the copied accounts in Matthew to make it seem like those accounts were written by the created disciple
- Emphasized Peter throughout the NT, for example:
    - o "But go, tell his disciples and Peter, 'He goes before you into Galilee. There you will see him, as he said to you.'" (Mark 16:7)
    - o They rose up that very hour, returned to Jerusalem, and found the eleven gathered together, and those who were with them, saying, "The Lord is risen indeed, and has appeared to Simon!" (Luke 24:33–34)
    - o "In these days, Peter stood up in the middle of the disciples (and the number of names was about one hundred twenty), and said," (Acts 1:15)
    - o "they were cut to the heart, and said to Peter and the rest of the disciples" (Acts 2:37)
    - o "But Peter and the apostles answered," (Acts 5:29)
    - o Then after three years I went up to Jerusalem to visit Peter, and stayed with him fifteen days. (Galatians 1:18)
    - o but to the contrary, when they saw that I had been entrusted with the Good News for the uncircumcised, even as Peter with the Good News for the circumcised—(Galatians 2:7)
- Created ART theology to hide the edits and fraud of the beast in the end time so that nobody will ever learn the truth:
    - o Interpreted Daniel 9:27 to be a seven-year end time great tribulation period rather than the most perfect prophecy about Jesus ever written

- o Edited the Olivet Discourse in Matthew to support end time ART second coming theology
- o Included Paul's words in the Bible so that the beast's leaders would have authority to speak for God just like Paul, a religious leader who also never met Jesus
- o Dated Revelation in the late first century to prevent Andrew and Peter from being recognized as the two witnesses, causing the two witnesses to be predicted to come at the end time

The NC coup by the beast was a well-thought-out and planned attack on the NC. Certainly, there is much more fraud, deceit, and editing that went into their NC coup.

John and the other eyewitnesses were led astray and fooled into selecting false teachers to replace them, and these antichrists worked with Satan to take complete control of the NC for 1300 years. Then, with 1000 years and an end time left, Jesus returned to free the Gospel from their control. But the effects of the beast remained and still are prevalent throughout the NC even today.

MIRACLE EYEWITNESS AND FRAUD JESUS EVIDENCE

1. Jesus is God born as a man with a mission to start the NC (6 BC)
2. Satan attempted to stop the NC from starting (6 BC)
3. Jesus' mission to teach, heal and perform miracles (26–30 AD)
    a. Mark 6:45–52 and John 6:16–26—James and John witnessed the miracle of Jesus' walking on water and calming a storm
4. Jesus' sacrifice and resurrection (30 AD)
5. Second half of Jesus' seven-year mission (30–33 AD)
6. Start of the NC, the Great Tribulation, and the AOD (33 AD)
7. Generation of the Disciples (33–67 AD)
8. The NC (33–2333 AD)
9. First half of the NC—the reign of the Beast (33–1333 AD)
    a. Matthew 16:12–21—False teachers edited Nicodemus' copy of James' observation of this event to create Jesus assigning Peter to reign over the NC on their behalf

b. Matthew 14:22–32—False teachers edited the account of Jesus walking on water by adding Matthew 14:28–31 that describes Peter also walking on water

c. Mark 5:36–43, 9:2–4, 14:32–42—ECFs edited Andrew out of being one of Jesus' inner circle disciples to elevate Peter's standing among the disciples

d. Matthew 9:9–11—ECFs edited a copied version of the tax collector story to claim Matthew as the author of the Gospel of Nicodemus

e. Matthew 10:2–4 and Mark 3:14–19—ECFs inserted a list of the twelve disciples in Mark, copied it into Matthew, and noted that Matthew was the tax collector

f. ECFs edited many copied verses in the Gospel of Matthew to have it appear as though their created author, Matthew, observed the events

g. ECFs made numerous edits to NT documentation to emphasize Peter and separate him from the rest of the disciples (e.g., Mark 16:7, Luke 24:33–34, etc.)

h. ECFs inserted Saul's letters into the Bible to give the beast leaders authority to speak for God, just like they claimed Saul had. ECFs and RCLs created theology to hide the deceit of the false teachers (e.g., ART, Daniel 9:27 to be the great tribulation, John dying in prison at an old age, etc.)

10. Second half of Jesus' NC—Jesus' 1000-year reign with his chosen ones (1333–2333 AD)

11. The Time of the End (2333-?)

12. Judgement

17

Jesus' Miracles

THERE ARE THREE EYEWITNESSES who provided their testimony documenting their observations of Jesus—Nicodemus [Gospel of Matthew], James [Gospel of Mark], and John [Gospel of John]. It's time to turn to the final pieces of evidence needed to complete this investigation—to prove Jesus' miracles, including his resurrection. I closely examined the miracle of Jesus walking on the water (Matthew 14:22–32, Mark 6:45–52, and John 6:16–26) and found that two of the three authors, James and John, were present to document their testimony. Therefore, the two- or three-witness requirement specified in Deuteronomy 17:6 and 19:15 was met for Jesus to have calmed a storm and walked on water. But since there is so much riding on the truth of Jesus, I decided to examine one more miracle to see if it could also be proven truthful by at least two of the three eyewitnesses.

Since most of Jesus' works were copied from James by Nicodemus, the best chance of proving another miracle is through a miracle presented in all three witness statements. There are many miracles documented by James that were copied by Nicodemus, but not many that were documented by all three authors. One miracle documented in all three Gospels that stands out from the rest is when Jesus is documented as having fed five thousand men from five loaves of bread and two fish (Matthew 14:15–21, Mark 6:35–45, and John 6:4–15). I fully expect to find that the secret disciple Nicodemus was not present and copied this event from James, and that John and James present similar accounts with different observational details.

Analyzing this event through the same process used for previous events provides the following individual actions with their analysis:

1. A CROWD WITH NO FOOD

Matthew 14:15
15 When evening had come, his disciples came to him, saying, "This place is deserted, and the hour is already late. Send the multitudes away, that they may go into the villages, and buy themselves food."

Mark 6:35–37
35 When it was late in the day, his disciples came to him and said, "This place is deserted, and it is late in the day.
36 Send them away, that they may go into the surrounding country and villages and buy themselves bread, for they have nothing to eat."

John 6:4–6
4 Now the Passover, the feast of the Jews, was at hand.
5 Jesus therefore, lifting up his eyes and seeing that a great multitude was coming to him, said to Philip, "Where are we to buy bread, that these may eat?"
6 He said this to test him, for he himself knew what he would do.

Analysis: The same details are presented in Matthew and Mark with some rearrangement and wording differences. It's easy to conclude already that, as expected, Nicodemus copied James' account with false teachers making some minor edits to it to make it seem as though it was written by an eyewitness named Matthew. James and John each described what they observed, and as expected, their accounts are a bit different. John noticed Jesus "lifting up his eyes" to see the large crowd prior to Jesus asking Philip what to do about the lack of food to feed them. James did not hear this discussion. John also noted that Jesus had 'tested' Philip because Jesus knew what Philip was going to do. Jesus either confided in John or John knew Jesus so well that he could read the situation as it unfolded. James is considering sending people on their way to get food, but he notices that it was late in the day and there was nowhere to eat in the deserted place they were at. Jesus' interaction with Philip is not even mentioned by James; therefore, the twelve disciples are split up; they are not together in one group.

2. JESUS RESPONDS

Matthew 14:16
16 But Jesus said to them, "They don't need to go away. You give them something to eat."

Mark 6:37
[37] But he answered them, "You give them something to eat."

Analysis: Again, the same details are presented in Matthew and Mark with some rearrangement. Nicodemus has copied from James, and the false teachers did some slight word-smithing to make it seem as though the author of the Gospel of Matthew was also present. John did not record this exchange between Jesus and this other group of disciples because he wasn't with them.

3. THE DISCIPLES RESPOND TO JESUS

Matthew 14:17
[17] They told him, "We only have here five loaves and two fish."

Mark 6:37–38
[37] They asked him, "Shall we go and buy two hundred denarii worth of bread and give them something to eat?" [38] He said to them, "How many loaves do you have? Go see." When they knew, they said, "Five, and two fish."

John 6:7–9
[7] Philip answered him, "Two hundred denarii worth of bread is not sufficient for them, that every one of them may receive a little." [8] One of his disciples, Andrew, Simon Peter's brother, said to him, [9] "There is a boy here who has five barley loaves and two fish, but what are these among so many?"

Analysis: Matthew is again a copy that leaves off many of the details presented in Mark. Therefore, Nicodemus is confirmed as not being present to witness this event. I'll omit Matthew from further analysis because it isn't necessary.

The key point made in James is the statement "When they knew. . ." James, with some other disciples, found out later that Jesus had five loaves and two fish to feed the 5000 with. James and the disciples who were with him did not witness the boy with the fish and loaves. John, Philip, and Andrew were separated from the other group of disciples because they witnessed Jesus' interaction with the boy who had the five loaves of bread and the two fish. Note that Andrew was with John to witness JB when they first started to follow Jesus, and he is again hanging around with John. John and Andrew were friends who hung around each other, and John was close to Jesus; therefore, so was Andrew. This is certainly additional proof that Andrew was one of the inner circle disciples.

4. JESUS GIVES DIRECTIONS AND TAKES ACTION

> Mark 6:39–42
> [39] He commanded them that everyone should sit down in groups
> on the green grass. [40] They sat down in ranks, by hundreds and
> by fifties. [41] He took the five loaves and the two fish; and looking
> up to heaven, he blessed and broke the loaves, and he gave to his
> disciples to set before them, and he divided the two fish among
> them all. [42] They all ate and were filled.

> John 6:10–11
> [10] Jesus said, "Have the people sit down." Now there was much
> grass in that place. So the men sat down, in number about five
> thousand. [11] Jesus took the loaves, and having given thanks, he
> distributed to the disciples, and the disciples to those who were
> sitting down, likewise also of the fish as much as they desired.

Analysis: The accounts of James and John are more similar now, indicating that the disciples are likely now in one group, but they provided different details of the same occurrence. James heard Jesus' command the disciples to have the crowd "sit down in groups," but John only heard Jesus command them to "Have the people sit down." James then described how people split up, sat on the green grass, and then how Jesus looked up to heaven as he blessed and broke the loaves. John was not concerned with these details because he was observant of the big picture and estimated the total number of people present. James and John noticed that Jesus blessed both the loaves and the fish together, then had the disciples distribute them.

5. CLOSING TIME

> Mark 6:43–45
> [43] They took up twelve baskets full of broken pieces and also of the
> fish. [44] Those who ate the loaves were five thousand men. [45] Imme-
> diately he made his disciples get into the boat and go ahead to the
> other side, to Bethsaida, while he himself sent the multitude away.

John 6:12–15
[12] When they were filled, he said to his disciples, "Gather up the broken pieces which are left over, that nothing be lost." [13] So they gathered them up, and filled twelve baskets with broken pieces from the five barley loaves, which were left over by those who had eaten. [14] When therefore the people saw the sign which Jesus did, they said, "This is truly the prophet who comes into the world." [15] Jesus, therefore, perceiving that they were about to come and take him by force to make him king, withdrew again to the mountain by himself.

Analysis: John and James both captured how much bread and fish were left over, but only John heard Jesus' command the disciples to collect the leftovers. John also provided a description of the reaction of those in the crowd. To end this event, James and John both described what they observed happened next from their own perspective. Putting the two accounts together describes all the details of how the event ended. Jesus sent the disciples away in a boat to Bethsaida, while Jesus went up the mountain again by himself to avoid the crowd taking him by force to make him king.

James and John were two eyewitnesses who were present to witness this miracle performed by Jesus to feed 5000 men from five loaves of bread and two fish obtained from a boy in the crowd. John's and James' stories match, but each has presented additional information beyond what the other presented, indicating their presence to observe the event and provide their eyewitness testimony. Had John not provided his testimony, we would not have details of Philip's interaction with Jesus, Andrew finding the boy with the loaves and fish, and the reaction of the crowd afterward. Had James not provided his eyewitness testimony, we would not be able to visualize how the crowd separated and sat in groups, how Jesus looked up to heaven as he blessed the meal, nor how Jesus sent the disciples in a boat to Bethsaida.

We now have two or three eyewitnesses who have twice validated Jesus performing miracles. I say two or three eyewitnesses because there are two solid eyewitnesses who were there, James and John, but Nicodemus copied James' account into his testimony, indicating that he believed what James witnessed. Two witnesses observed Jesus calming a storm and walking on water and feeding 5000 men with five loaves of bread and two fish, and Nicodemus wasn't present but he copied them both because he believed.

Next up for analysis is the most important miracle of all—Jesus' resurrection, but first, the summary of eyewitness documentation from this analysis is again presented.

MORE MIRACLE EYEWITNESS JESUS EVIDENCE

1. Jesus is God born as a man with a mission to start the NC (6 BC)
2. Satan attempted to stop the NC from starting (6 BC)
3. Jesus' mission to teach, heal and perform miracles (26–30 AD)
    a. Mark 6:35–45, and John 6:4–15—James and John, two eyewitnesses who were present, observed Jesus' miracle to feed 5000 with five loaves of bread and two fish
    b. Matthew 14:15–21—Nicodemus again copied an account from James (feeding 5000) indicating that he believed what James wrote was factual
    c. John 6:7–9—The disciples are split up, and Andrew was again with John, who was with Jesus, proving that Andrew was close to Jesus and was an inner circle disciple
4. Jesus' sacrifice and resurrection (30 AD)
5. Second half of Jesus' seven-year mission (30–33 AD)
6. Start of the NC, the Great Tribulation, and the AOD (33 AD)
7. Generation of the Disciples (33–67 AD)
8. The NC (33–2333 AD)
9. First half of the NC—the reign of the Beast (33–1333 AD)
10. Second half of Jesus' NC—Jesus' 1000-year reign with his chosen ones (1333–2333 AD)
11. The Time of the End (2333-?)
12. Judgement

18

An Execution and Resurrection

THE ONE MAJOR ATTRIBUTE of Jesus left to prove is the resurrection miracle that separates Jesus from the claims of all other men and women. To prove a resurrection, there must first be proof that the resurrected person had died. That simple fact reminds me of the story of Sai Baba, provided to me by an atheist who told me that Jesus' resurrection wasn't from God because others had also resurrected dead people back to life. I asked for and received a summary that was claimed to be evidence proving that Sai Baba resurrected a person from the dead. The summary was second-hand or even less reliable information that was assembled to make it look as though Sai Baba resurrected someone from the dead. But there was no eyewitness testimony that the person had died or had been resurrected by Sai Baba.

I've been through a long process proving that there are three eyewitnesses who documented their testimony about Jesus. The next step is to examine their documentation to determine if they witnessed Jesus die and then later resurrect himself from the dead. But first, I need convincing documentation that Jesus died:

1. THE FINAL HOURS

> Matthew 27:45–47
> [45] Now from the sixth hour there was darkness over all the land until the ninth hour. [46] About the ninth hour, Jesus cried with a loud voice, saying, "Eli, Eli, lima sabachthani?" That is, "My God, my God, why have you forsaken me?" [47] Some of them who stood there, when they heard it, said, "This man is calling Elijah."

Mark 15:33–35
[33] When the sixth hour had come, there was darkness over the
whole land until the ninth hour. [34] At the ninth hour, Jesus cried
with a loud voice, saying, "Eloi, Eloi, lama sabachthani?" which is,
being interpreted, "My God, my God, why have you forsaken me?"
[35] Some of those who stood by, when they heard it, said, "Behold,
he is calling Elijah."

John 19:25–27
[25] But standing by Jesus' cross were his mother, his mother's sister,
Mary the wife of Clopas, and Mary Magdalene. [26] Therefore when
Jesus saw his mother, and the disciple whom he loved standing
there, he said to his mother, "Woman, behold, your son!" [27] Then
he said to the disciple, "Behold, your mother!" From that hour, the
disciple took her to his own home.

Analysis: Very quickly, I can see that Nicodemus was not present to witness Jesus' execution because he copied Jesus' execution from James. James and John provided different details of what was happening at the foot of the cross; therefore, we know they were both present to observe Jesus' execution. James Zebedee noted that the world became dark as the light of the world was being extinguished on the cross. Also, James captured the words of Jesus and the reaction of those who were at the execution site. John's attention is on Jesus and the women who are there at the cross. John also notes that even though Jesus had several brothers (Mark 6:3), Jesus commanded John to take care of his mother, and John stated that he did as commanded. None of Jesus' brothers are documented at the cross, and Jesus didn't choose any of his brothers as disciples. Jesus chose John to take care of his mother, indicating that none of his brothers were trustworthy. These details were provided by the Holy Spirit to have you reject the false teacher-created story that Jesus' brother James became a follower of Jesus and a leader in the early church. With James, Jesus' brother, as an "apostle," Paul and the others gained credibility for being called "apostles" who, like James, could be claimed to be speaking for God. Much more on this concept will be presented in the analysis of the resurrection accounts. The observations of John and James, when combined, provide the complete story of how Jesus was executed.

2. JESUS' FINAL WORDS

Matthew 27:48–50
[48] Immediately one of them ran and took a sponge, filled it with vinegar, put it on a reed, and gave him a drink. [49] The rest said, "Let him be. Let's see whether Elijah comes to save him." [50] Jesus cried again with a loud voice, and yielded up his spirit.

Mark 15:36–37
[36] One ran, and filling a sponge full of vinegar, put it on a reed and gave it to him to drink, saying, "Let him be. Let's see whether Elijah comes to take him down." [37] Jesus cried out with a loud voice and gave up the spirit.

John 19:28–30
[28] After this, Jesus, seeing that all things were now finished, that the Scripture might be fulfilled, said, "I am thirsty!" [29] Now a vessel full of vinegar was set there; so they put a sponge full of the vinegar on hyssop, and held it at his mouth. [30] When Jesus therefore had received the vinegar, he said, "It is finished!" Then he bowed his head and gave up his spirit.

Analysis: Nicodemus is still not at the cross or nearby to witness Jesus' death. John observed Jesus stating that "I am thirsty," and James and John both noted that vinegar was offered to Jesus. John noted that Jesus "received the vinegar," from a "vessel full of vinegar" that was set there and James noticed the one giving Jesus vinegar mocked Jesus. Both James and John witnessed Jesus' death, but John, with his eyes on Jesus, noted Jesus' final words and recorded them, while James heard Jesus' shout but didn't catch his last words. John, again with his eyes on Jesus, noted that Jesus "bowed his head," then both James and John describe how Jesus died by giving up his spirit. The difference in eyewitness observation details proves them both to be at the cross to confirm Jesus' death.

3. WHAT HAPPENED NEXT

Matthew 27:51–53
[51] Behold, the veil of the temple was torn in two from the top to the bottom. The earth quaked and the rocks were split. [52] The tombs were opened, and many bodies of the saints who had fallen asleep were raised; [53] and coming out of the tombs after his resurrection, they entered into the holy city and appeared to many.

Mark 15:38–41
[38] The veil of the temple was torn in two from the top to the bottom. [39] When the centurion, who stood by opposite him, saw that
he cried out like this and breathed his last, he said, "Truly this man
was the Son of God! [40] There were also women watching from afar,
among whom were both Mary Magdalene and Mary the mother
of James the less and of Joses, and Salome; [41] who, when he was
in Galilee, followed him and served him; and many other women
who came up with him to Jerusalem.

John 19:31–35
[31] Therefore the Jews, because it was the Preparation Day, so that
the bodies wouldn't remain on the cross on the Sabbath (for that
Sabbath was a special one), asked of Pilate that their legs might be
broken and that they might be taken away. [32] Therefore the soldiers came and broke the legs of the first and of the other who was
crucified with him; [33] but when they came to Jesus and saw that he
was already dead, they didn't break his legs. [34] However, one of the
soldiers pierced his side with a spear, and immediately blood and
water came out. [35] He who has seen has testified, and his testimony
is true. He knows that he tells the truth, that you may believe.

Analysis: Nicodemus is not at the cross, so he is likely near the temple and could have witnessed what was happening there and documented it. In his book, it is written that the earth quaked, rocks split, the veil of the temple was torn in two, and saints were resurrected and made appearances. Only one of those details is confirmed in Mark—the veil of the temple was torn in two," but James is at the cross, so he couldn't have witnessed this. There are additional concerns with the account in Mark. First, the comment about the veil is out of place because James couldn't have witnessed this. Then the account contradicts John's account and states that the women whom John has placed at the cross were watching from afar. John's account makes sense that the woman who loved Jesus would be at the cross with John, so they would not be watching from afar. The comment in Mark about the centurion stating at Jesus' death that "Truly this man was the Son of God!" indicates that this centurion is likely the one whom Jesus healed his servant (Mark 8:5–13). Everything else in this section of Mark makes no sense; therefore, just like this section in Matthew, it has been corrupted by false teachers. These facts indicate that the outrageous claims in Nicodemus' account that are not validated in the others could be false teachers embellishing the death of Jesus. John and James were at the cross and noticed Jesus breathe his last breath, then only

John recorded what happened next, except for the comment in Mark that had James describing the actions of the Centurion.

4. THE BODY IS REQUESTED

Matthew 27:57–58
[57] When evening had come, a rich man from Arimathaea named Joseph, who himself was also Jesus' disciple, came. [58] This man went to Pilate and asked for Jesus' body. Then Pilate commanded the body to be given up.

Mark 15:42–45
[42] When evening had now come, because it was the Preparation Day, that is, the day before the Sabbath, [43] Joseph of Arimathaea, a prominent council member who also himself was looking for God's Kingdom, came. He boldly went in to Pilate, and asked for Jesus' body. [44] Pilate was surprised to hear that he was already dead; and summoning the centurion, he asked him whether he had been dead long. [45] When he found out from the centurion, he granted the body to Joseph.

John 19:38–39
[38] After these things, Joseph of Arimathaea, being a disciple of Jesus, but secretly for fear of the Jews, asked of Pilate that he might take away Jesus' body. Pilate gave him permission. He came therefore and took away his body. [39] Nicodemus, who at first came to Jesus by night, also came bringing a mixture of myrrh and aloes, about a hundred Roman pounds.

Analysis: Two of the three eyewitnesses, James and John, have observed Jesus' death on the cross, but our third witness, Nicodemus, had not. The evening of Jesus' death on preparation day—the day before the Sabbath, Jesus' body was requested from Pilate by a man named Joseph, who was:

a. *"a rich man. . . who himself was also Jesus' disciple—Matthew [Nicodemus]*

b. *"a prominent council member who also was looking for God's Kingdom"—Mark [James*

c. *"a disciple of Jesus, but secretly for fear of the Jews"—John*

James' account appears to be copied by Nicodemus, but the extra eyewitness detail in Nicodemus' account indicates he was present, and John has validated Nicodemus joining Joseph at the scene at some point. Nicodemus' account in Matthew is expected to be the one with all the details, but it isn't—it is James' account that provides the eyewitness testimony for obtaining the body. James is not expected to be there. Has there been false teacher tampering? John knew Nicodemus who was a religious leader so it is possible he also knew Joseph. James knew Nicodemus and also possibly knew Joseph. At any rate, John placed Nicodemus at the scene, and Nicodemus is expected to be there. Therefore, it's most likely that the details about Joseph in these accounts came from Nicodemus. John's account of Nicodemus joining with Joseph to entomb Jesus' body provides eyewitness details of the herbs, and Nicodemus would not have documented his testimony had he not witnessed Jesus dead and resurrected. Therefore, false teacher editing to remove Nicodemus as the author prevents me from confirming Nicodemus witnessed Jesus' death, but it is probable from the documentation.

EVIDENCE OF JESUS DYING

1. Jesus is God born as a man with a mission to start the NC (6 BC)
2. Satan attempted to stop the NC from starting (6 BC)
3. Jesus' mission to teach, heal and perform miracles (26–30 AD)
4. Jesus' sacrifice and resurrection (30 AD)
    a. John 19:25–27—Jesus assigned his mother to John, indicating that Jesus' brothers, including James, were not disciples of Jesus nor would they follow him later
    b. Matthew 27:48–50, Mark 15:36–37, John 19:28–30—Two eyewitnesses, James and John, recorded Jesus dying on the cross; he said his last words and gave up his spirit and Nicodemus copied it from James indicating that he believed Jesus died
    c. Matthew 27:51–53, Mark 15:38–41, John 19:31–35—There is evidence of tampering with James' and Nicodemus' accounts of what happened after Jesus' death
    d. John 19:38–39—Nicodemus is documented with Joseph entombing Jesus' body; therefore, he witnessed Jesus as having died on the cross

5. Second half of Jesus' seven-year mission (30–33 AD)
6. Start of the NC, the Great Tribulation, and the AOD (33 AD)
7. Generation of the Disciples (33–67 AD)
8. The NC (33–2333 AD)
9. First half of the NC—the reign of the Beast (33–1333 AD)
10. Second half of Jesus' NC—Jesus' 1000-year reign with his chosen ones (1333–2333 AD)
11. The Time of the End (2333-?)
12. Judgement

19

A Resurrection Miracle—Part 1

Of all the miracles documented in the Gospels, I finally get to the analysis of the most important one—the resurrection of Jesus. We have a proven death, now I am going to take a forensic look at the resurrection accounts. With a proven resurrection, Jesus' claims to be God are valid. Without a proven resurrection, Jesus was just a great man.

The analysis of the resurrection documentation to determine the truth is not an easy task because:

- There are numerous accounts presented in the Gospels, including the Gospel of Luke—the second-hand or worse testimony, but all of them, including those in Luke, must be examined,
- False teacher edits have clearly affected the integrity of Bible documentation, so I will have to wade through the accounts knowing that each may have been corrupted by false teachers, and,
- There are additional "appearances" documented in one of Saul's letters and the book of Acts that must also be considered.

In summary, there are twelve discrete Gospel resurrection accounts to be examined:

1. Two Women—Mary Magdalene and the Other Mary (Matthew 28:7–10)
2. The Disciples at a Mountain in Galilee (Matthew 28:16–20)
3. First Appeared to Mary Magdalene (Mark 16:9–11 and John 20:14–18)
4. Two Men on the Road (Mark 16:12–13 and Luke 24:13–32)

5. The Disciples (Luke 24:35–53 and John 20:19–23)
6. Sitting at a Table (Mark 16:14–20)
7. The Disciples with Thomas (John 20:26–29)
8. Seven Disciples at the Sea of Tiberias (John 21:1–23)
9. Saul's Claim for Peter, James, and the Apostles (1 Corinthians 15:3–8)
10. Saul, Also Called Paul (Acts 9:3–20, 22:6–16, and 26:12–18)
11. Jesus Appears to Others Over Forty Days (Acts 1:3)
12. Jesus Appears to "them" Likely on Mount Olivet (Acts 1:4–9)

The resurrection account analysis is long and complex; therefore, I've split it into four sections. First, I'll focus on the Gospel accounts 1–4, then Part 2 will address 5–8, followed by Part 3 of the analysis that addresses Saul's accounts 9–10. Finally, I'll present the analysis of the Acts resurrection events 11–12, with the first requiring extensive analysis with an exceptional conclusion.

Forensically reviewing the documentation for each of these resurrection appearances, one at a time, reveals them to be either a valid account or a fabricated story created by false teachers to support their NC coup through Bible documentation edits.

1. TWO WOMEN—MARY MAGDALENE AND THE OTHER MARY (MATTHEW 28:7–10)

> Go quickly and tell his disciples, 'He has risen from the dead, and behold, he goes before you into Galilee; there you will see him.' Behold, I have told you." [8] They departed quickly from the tomb with fear and great joy, and ran to bring his disciples word. [9] As they went to tell his disciples, behold, Jesus met them, saying, "Rejoice!" They came and took hold of his feet, and worshiped him. [10] Then Jesus said to them, "Don't be afraid. Go tell my brothers that they should go into Galilee, and there they will see me." (Matthew 28:7–10)

Analysis: The account starts with an angel telling two women, "Mary Magdalene and the other Mary" (Matthew 28:1), to go and tell the disciples to go to Galilee, where they will see Jesus resurrected. Then, on the way to tell the disciples the account describes Jesus' meeting with them, saying, "Rejoice."

Jesus then gives the woman the same instructions to go and tell the disciples he will meet them in Galilee. There are four major issues with this account:

1. *The messages received by the woman to tell the disciples to go to Galilee to see Jesus resurrected contradict John's resurrection account that describes Jesus' first meeting with the disciples in a house that same day in Jerusalem (John 20:18–19).*
2. *There is no description of Jesus resurrected, and no details are provided about how Jesus appeared to them. What did Jesus look like? Could they see the wounds on Jesus from his execution? Did the women turn the corner to find Jesus standing in the middle of the path—or the side of the path? Did he fade in? This is supposed to be an account of someone witnessing a resurrection; therefore, every vivid detail would be burned into an eyewitness' brain. A person witnessing Jesus' resurrection would never forget the details, yet no eyewitness details are presented here.*
3. *The muted reaction stating that the women "took hold of his feet, and worshiped him" is a strange reaction with no details. Did they bend down? Did they fall? Did they both do this at the same time? They witnessed Jesus resurrected, yet apparently neither one had anything to say. This is not eyewitness testimony.*
4. *Then there is a major contradiction in this account with what is provided by James and John. James claimed that Jesus "appeared first to Mary Magdalene" (Mark 16:9), and John validated this (John 20:16–17). The accounts by James and John don't mention Jesus' meeting with two women. If there were two women, the details would surely have been presented by both James and John, too. There is zero chance that Mary told the story and left out the fact that there was another woman with her.*

In summary, there are no situational eyewitness details that validate this story as truthful, and it contradicts other accounts. For these reasons, I am confident in claiming that Matthew 28:7–10 is not eyewitness testimony; it is a false teacher fabrication.

2. THE DISCIPLES AT A MOUNTAIN IN GALILEE (MATTHEW 28:16–20)

> [16] But the eleven disciples went into Galilee, to the mountain
> where Jesus had sent them. [17] When they saw him, they bowed
> down to him, but some doubted. [18] Jesus came to them and spoke
> to them, saying, "All authority has been given to me in heaven and
> on earth. [19] Go and make disciples of all nations, baptizing them
> in the name of the Father and of the Son and of the Holy Spirit,
> [20] teaching them to observe all things that I commanded you. Behold, I am with you always, even to the end of the age." Amen. (Matthew 28:16–20)

Analysis: My first impression is that this summary was written to validate the previous resurrection account of the two Marys being told by the angel and Jesus to tell the disciples to meet Jesus resurrected in Galilee. As already stated, those documented directions don't make sense because Jesus will first meet the disciples in Jerusalem. There are additional issues with this account:

1. *Again, there is no description of what Jesus looked like.*
2. *The disciples had nothing to say. When was Peter ever silent?*
3. *John wrote that, as expected, after the disciples witnessed Jesus resurrected, they believed (John 2:22). This account states that the disciples witnessed Jesus resurrected, "but some doubted." Who doubted and why?*
4. *The entire account lacks situational eyewitness details.*

In summary, this resurrection account is clearly not eyewitness testimony, and with its connection to the directions to go to Galilee, I consider it to also be a false teacher fabrication. In fact, the last portion of the account seems like it was written by ECFs to support the passed-down disciple authority to the Catholic Church per Catechism #880.

In summary, both resurrection accounts presented in the Gospel of Matthew are false teacher edits. Nicodemus, as a religious leader and ruler, knew the eyewitness testimony requirements from Deuteronomy. Nicodemus witnessed Jesus' resurrection; otherwise, he wouldn't have documented his testimony. Therefore, even though these accounts in his book are fabrications, I expect to find Nicodemus's eyewitness account of Jesus resurrected.

3. FIRST APPEARED TO MARY MAGDALENE (MARK 16:9–11 AND JOHN 20:14–18)

> 9 Now when he had risen early on the first day of the week, he appeared first to Mary Magdalene, from whom he had cast out seven demons. 10 She went and told those who had been with him, as they mourned and wept. 11 When they heard that he was alive and had been seen by her, they disbelieved. (Mark 16:9–11)

Analysis: James has testified that he witnessed Mary Magdalene claiming to be the first person to have witnessed Jesus resurrected. James didn't record her testimony, and he claimed that he and the other disciples did not believe her story. James' story makes sense. The disciples had been with Jesus almost 3-1/2 years from the beginning of his ministry, so certainly they expected Jesus to appear to them before a woman whom Jesus had "cast out seven demons." James' accounting of Jesus appearing to Mary is not enough to believe it happened because there is no eyewitness testimony from Mary presented.

But that is fixed because John recorded Mary's testimony that James heard:

> 14 When she had said this, she turned around and saw Jesus standing, and didn't know that it was Jesus. 15 Jesus said to her, "Woman, why are you weeping? Who are you looking for?" She, supposing him to be the gardener, said to him, "Sir, if you have carried him away, tell me where you have laid him, and I will take him away." 16 Jesus said to her, "Mary." She turned and said to him, "Rabboni!" which is to say, "Teacher!" 17 Jesus said to her, "Don't hold me, for I haven't yet ascended to my Father; but go to my brothers and tell them, 'I am ascending to my Father and your Father, to my God and your God.'" 18 Mary Magdalene came and told the disciples that she had seen the Lord, and that he had said these things to her. (John 20:14–18)

Analysis: Prior to this event, John recorded that he and Peter witnessed Mary Magdalene running from where Jesus' body had been laid to tell them the tomb of Jesus was empty (John 20:1–2). They all ran to the tomb, and Peter and John also found it to be empty (John 20:3–10). In support of this being eyewitness testimony, John recorded numerous situational details he observed at the tomb, such as:

- *John "outran Peter and came to the tomb first."*
- *An exact description of Jesus' burial cloths—"the cloth that had been on his head, not lying with the linen cloths, but rolled up in a place by itself."*

John's eyewitness details place him with Mary Magdalene that morning, and his details verify the empty tomb. Then John recorded that Peter and John left and went home, while Mary remained outside the tomb, weeping (John 20:11). Then she witnessed two angels in the tomb who spoke with her (John 20:12–13). Afterward, she witnessed Jesus resurrected, and we get a description of what she saw and what they discussed (John 20:14–17). Then she ran and told the disciples what had happened (John 20:18). John recorded the situational details that Mary presented:

- *"Mary was standing outside at the tomb, weeping"*
- *"she wept, she stooped and looked into the tomb"*
- *"she saw two angels in white sitting, one at the head and one at the feet, where the body of Jesus had lain."*
- *"When she had said this, she turned around and saw Jesus standing, and didn't know that it was Jesus."*
- *"She, supposing him to be the gardener" asked him where Jesus' body was?*
- *" Jesus said to her, 'Mary.'"*
- *"She turned and said to him, 'Rabboni!' which is to say, 'Teacher!'"*

Mary knew Jesus, but she did not immediately recognize him; she stated he looked like the "gardener." Jesus was disguised from being recognized, and this is a very important piece of evidence in proving resurrection accounts to be valid or fiction. Jesus in disguise is testimony from God—Jesus himself, that he has been resurrected.

John, through eyewitness details, has placed himself at the tomb and present with Mary to hear her account, leading up to the details she provided of Jesus' resurrection. James has validated that the disciples heard Mary Magdalene's story, and John recorded the details of it. There are eyewitness details presented of the appearance, and Jesus is in disguise, fulfilling the role of a second witness. In summary, there are two witnesses—Mary Magdalene, who provided her testimony of Jesus resurrected, with Jesus as a second witness. Her testimony was recorded by John and validated by James. Based on this evidence, Mary Magdalene was the first to witness Jesus resurrected from the dead.

In closing, note the following contradictions of this account when compared to the fictional one presented in Matthew:

a. *Jesus appeared only to Mary Magdalene and not to two women,*

b. *The appearance to Mary Magdalene was at the tomb of Jesus, not on the way back to the disciples after Mary Magdalene and the other Mary had left the tomb, and,*

c. *Jesus did not tell Mary to tell the disciples to go to Galilee.*

4. TWO MEN ON THE ROAD (MARK 16:12–13 AND LUKE 24:13–32)

> [12] After these things, he was revealed in another form to two of them, as they walked on their way into the country. [13] They went away and told it to the rest. They didn't believe them, either. (Mark 16:9–13)

Analysis: Again, James is not testifying that he witnessed Jesus resurrected; he is testifying that two witnesses TOLD him and "the rest" that they observed and witnessed Jesus resurrected. The account is written as though at least one of the two men was one of the twelve disciples because they met up with "the rest," which will be stated to be a locked room, to provide their testimony. The disciples were hiding from the Jews, but these two men knew where they were. Deuteronomy 17:6 and 19:15 require two witnesses to testify to have them believe, and the disciples have now heard Mary Magdalene and these two men, but they still didn't believe. They won't believe until they witness Jesus resurrected (John 2:22). Hence, Jesus' comment that those who do not see but believe are blessed (John 20:29).

Then we turn to the Gospel of Luke, the second-hand Gospel for supporting testimony:

> [13] Behold, two of them were going that very day to a village named Emmaus, which was sixty stadia from Jerusalem. [14] They talked with each other about all of these things that had happened. [15] While they talked and questioned together, Jesus himself came near and went with them. [16] But their eyes were kept from recognizing him. [17] He said to them, "What are you talking about as you walk, and are sad?" [18] One of them, named Cleopas, answered him, "Are you the only stranger in Jerusalem who doesn't know the things which have happened there in these days?" (Luke 24:13–18)

Analysis: The author told us where they were going, what they were talking about, and the name of one of the men who was present. Most importantly, the eyewitnesses knew Jesus because initially "their eyes were kept from recognizing him." Even though this account is presented in a Gospel written by an anonymous author who claimed not to be an eyewitness to Jesus, there are eyewitness details presented that support James' claim of the two men. Therefore, I need to consider it:

> [30] When he had sat down at the table with them, he took the bread
> and gave thanks. Breaking it, he gave it to them. [31] Their eyes were
> opened and they recognized him; then he vanished out of their
> sight. [32] They said to one another, "Weren't our hearts burning
> within us while he spoke to us along the way, and while he opened
> the Scriptures to us?"

Consider how odd it is to have two men witness Jesus resurrected—a one-time event—but then only record the name of one of them. This is Jesus' second recorded resurrection appearance, and it is BEFORE Jesus appeared to the rest of the disciples. Jesus went out of his way to ensure that we know the names of both men, and at least one of them is a disciple of Jesus. In the days and even years that followed, everyone knew who that second man was. Therefore, we can be assured that the name of this second man was recorded in the Gospel testimonies that were completed by 33 AD. This can only mean one thing—the name of that second man was intentionally removed. False teachers did not want you knowing the name of the second man Jesus appeared to because it was damaging to their claim to own and control the NC.

Recall that the resurrection accounts in Nicodemus' Gospel [Matthew] are fictitious and Nicodemus would not have documented his testimony if he hadn't witnessed Jesus resurrected. There is only one man who fits the profile to be that second man that Jesus appeared to, that false teachers want hidden from the world—Nicodemus.

Jesus started teaching Nicodemus that first night when Nicodemus went to meet Jesus, and John recorded the details. We can be assured that during this resurrection appearance, Jesus is expanding on the teaching he had earlier provided Nicodemus. Recall that Jesus compared himself to Moses when they first met (John 3:14–15). At this appearance, Jesus taught Nicodemus about how Jesus had "to suffer these things" to fulfill the prophecy "from Moses and from all the prophets" (Luke 24:26–29). Then, just as it happened for Mary Magdalene, Nicodemus knew Jesus but didn't recognize him at first. Jesus revealed himself to him later (Luke 24:30–32). Just as Jesus appeared in disguise for Mary Magdalene, he has also appeared in disguise and then revealed himself to testify on his own behalf.

In summary, the account of the two men was written by Nicodemus and included in his book, then false teachers removed it and inserted it into the Gospel of Luke to attempt to validate that Gospel as proven testimony. Then they replaced Nicodemus' resurrection account with the resurrection accounts in Matthew, which are confirmed to be fictional. Just as we had for the account of Mary Magdalene, we have two witnesses for this event—Nicodemus and Jesus in disguise testifying on his own behalf. It has been validated by James, who stated that he and the rest of the disciples heard his testimony but didn't believe it. This resurrection account was also likely confirmed by John 7:53—8:11 in the section of his testimony that was conveniently lost by the false teachers. Furthermore, it will be apparent that John has confirmed this account through the next appearance of Jesus that was recorded.

DOCUMENTED RESURRECTION TESTIMONY

1. Jesus is God born as a man with a mission to start the NC (6 BC)
2. Satan attempted to stop the NC from starting (6 BC)
3. Jesus' mission to teach, heal and perform miracles (26–30 AD)
4. Jesus' sacrifice and resurrection (30 AD)
    a. Mark 16:9–11, John 20:14–18—Jesus appeared to Mary Magdalene and testified on his own behalf because he was hidden from view, then revealed himself later. John, who placed himself with Mary, documented her testimony that presents eyewitness situational details, and James validated that he heard Mary's testimony, so it is a valid testimony of Jesus' resurrection
    b. Mark 16:12–13, Luke 24:13–32—Jesus testified to this account because he was hidden from view and then revealed himself later. Nicodemus, as one of the two men, provided numerous eyewitness situational details, and James validated that he heard his testimony, so it is a valid testimony of Jesus' resurrection
5. Second half of Jesus' seven-year mission (30–33 AD)
6. Start of the NC, the Great Tribulation, and the AOD (33 AD)
7. Generation of the Disciples (33–67 AD)
8. The NC (33–2333 AD)

9. First half of the NC—the reign of the Beast (33–1333 AD)
    a. Matthew 28:7–10—This resurrection account has no situational eyewitness details, a muted reaction by those witnessing it, and it contradicts other resurrection accounts; therefore, it is a false teacher-created account
    b. Matthew 28:16–20—Clearly, a false teacher created an account to validate Matthew 28:7–10 because there is no description of Jesus, the eyewitnesses had nothing to say, the content contradicts John 2:22, and there are no situational eyewitness details
10. Second half of Jesus' NC—Jesus' 1000-year reign with his chosen ones (1333–2333 AD)
11. The Time of the End (2333-?)
12. Judgement

20

A Resurrection Miracle—Part 2

5. THE DISCIPLES (LUKE 24:33–49 AND JOHN 20:19–23)

> [33] They rose up that very hour, returned to Jerusalem, and found
> the eleven gathered together, and those who were with them, [34]
> saying, "The Lord is risen indeed, and has appeared to Simon!" [35]
> They related the things that happened along the way, and how he
> was recognized by them in the breaking of the bread. [36] As they
> said these things, Jesus himself stood among them, and said to
> them, "Peace be to you." (Luke 24:33–36)
>
> When, therefore, it was evening on that day, the first day of the week, and when the doors were locked where the disciples were assembled, for fear of the Jews, Jesus came and stood in the middle and said to them, "Peace be to you." (John 20:19)

Analysis: The two men on the road knew where to find the disciples because one of them was a disciple named Nicodemus. The account in Luke states that the two men returned to Jerusalem and "found the eleven gathered together," but this comment is not true. Three of the disciples, Nicodemus, Judas the traitor, and Thomas, were not present; therefore, the "eleven" could not be gathered there. Then the account claims that the two men found those there, saying, "The Lord is risen indeed, and has appeared to Simon." The introduction to this appearance, Luke 24:33–34, is clearly false teacher editing.

The two men showed up and told the disciples the details of Jesus' appearing to them, just as James wrote in Mark, then Nicodemus reported that "Jesus himself stood among them." John, as usual, provided eyewitness situational details. He described when this appearance happened and the fact that the "doors were locked" for "fear of the Jews." John's observations were the same as Nicodemus because the two eyewitnesses reported that Jesus "stood among them." Both Nicodemus and John reported hearing Jesus speak the same words when he appeared, "Peace be to you."

> [37] But they were terrified and filled with fear, and supposed that
> they had seen a spirit. [38] He said to them, "Why are you troubled?
> Why do doubts arise in your hearts? [39] See my hands and my feet,
> that it is truly me. Touch me and see, for a spirit doesn't have flesh
> and bones, as you see that I have." [40] When he had said this, he
> showed them his hands and his feet. (Luke 24:37–40)

> [20] When he had said this, he showed them his hands and his side.
> The disciples therefore were glad when they saw the Lord. (John 20:20)

Analysis: Jesus was initially hidden because Nicodemus reported they "supposed they had seen a spirit," and Jesus had to show them his "hands and feet." John confirms that Jesus was not recognized at first because he documented Jesus "showed them his hands and his feet," and after they saw this, they "were glad when they saw the Lord." The two accounts match, so there are three eyewitnesses: John, Nicodemus, and Jesus as his own witness because he had to reveal himself.

This happened while Nicodemus and Cleopas were providing their eyewitness testimony of Jesus' previous appearance to them. Therefore, it is likely that James documented this appearance of Jesus, but it didn't support John Mark writing the words of Peter, so false teachers removed his resurrection testimony and replaced it with Mark 16:14–20. I will analyze that resurrection account next. But first, wrapping up the details of this account, we have the following additional details:

> [41] While they still didn't believe for joy, and wondered, he said to
> them, "Do you have anything here to eat?" [42] They gave him a piece
> of a broiled fish and some honeycomb. [43] He took them and ate in
> front of them. [44] He said to them, "This is what I told you while I
> was still with you, that all things which are written in the law of
> Moses, the prophets, and the psalms concerning me must be fulfilled."
> [45] Then he opened their minds, that they might understand
> the Scriptures. [46] He said to them, "Thus it is written, and thus it
> was necessary for the Christ to suffer and to rise from the dead the
> third day, [47] and that repentance and remission of sins should be

preached in his name to all the nations, beginning at Jerusalem. (Luke 24:41–47)

> [21] Jesus therefore said to them again, "Peace be to you. As the Father has sent me, even so I send you." (John 20:21)

Analysis: What happened after Jesus revealed himself to the disciples is presented in both accounts. Nicodemus captures the details of how Jesus ate in the presence of the disciples, then explained to them how he fulfilled the scripture. Notice the repetition of Jesus' command that the Good News is to be "preached in his name TO ALL THE NATIONS." Nicodemus has documented himself as being commissioned by Jesus to document his testimony. John's description, "as the Father has sent me, even so I send you," is an abbreviated summary of what Nicodemus wrote.

> [48] You are witnesses of these things. [49] Behold, I send out the promise of my Father on you. (Luke 24:48–49)

> [22] When he had said this, he breathed on them, and said to them, "Receive the Holy Spirit! [23] If you forgive anyone's sins, they have been forgiven them. If you retain anyone's sins, they have been retained. (John 20:22–23)

Analysis: Both accounts then state that Jesus provided the disciples the Holy Spirit that Jesus had promised them (John 14:26–27). In summary, on the first day of Jesus' resurrection, he appeared to Mary Magdalene, Nicodemus, and Cleopas on the road, then to the disciples—Nicodemus included. All three appearances have been validated by Jesus, through him first appearing in disguise, then revealing himself so that we know them to be true.

6. SITTING AT A TABLE (MARK 16:14–20)

> [14] Afterward he was revealed to the eleven themselves as they sat at the table; and he rebuked them for their unbelief and hardness of heart, because they didn't believe those who had seen him after he had risen. [15] He said to them, "Go into all the world and preach the Good News to the whole creation. [16] He who believes and is baptized will be saved; but he who disbelieves will be condemned. [17] These signs will accompany those who believe: in my name they will cast out demons; they will speak with new languages; [18] they will take up serpents; and if they drink any deadly thing, it will in no way hurt them; they will lay hands on the sick, and they will

> recover." [19] So then the Lord, after he had spoken to them, was received up into heaven and sat down at the right hand of God. [20] They went out and preached everywhere, the Lord working with them and confirming the word by the signs that followed. Amen. (Mark 16:14–20)

Analysis: There is no description of what Jesus looked like, how the disciples responded, nor where this event took place. The false teachers again tried to validate this account by claiming "the eleven themselves" were present, but there are no eyewitness details presented indicating that this event occurred. James didn't close out his book with this summary after mentioning that he and the other disciples rejected the testimony of Mary Magdalene and the two men. He has been with the disciples on at least three separate occasions when they observed Jesus' resurrection, but none of those accounts are presented, John will confirm James presence at the resurrection appearance of Jesus at the Sea of Tiberias.

Note that the Gospel of Mark ends with a summary that is straight out of the CRL book of talking points. This account states that Jesus used the term "creation" to indicate people from the beginning, rather than the future. The term creation is a term favored by Paul to refer to spreading the word of God—e.g., four times in Romans 8:19–22, and many other references in his letters. The comments, "take up serpents. . .will in no way hurt them," and "lay hand on the sick, and they will recover," validate descriptions of Paul's events in the book of Acts (Acts 28:36 and 8–9). It's almost as though the ECFs that inserted that comment had help from Paul to write this account. If the disciples had observed that Jesus "sat down at the right hand of God," the account would contain details like John's vision in Revelation.

Whatever James wrote did not support John Mark writing the words of Peter, so it was removed and replaced with fiction. Some scholars believe that the ending of Mark is not trustworthy. For example, the New International Version claims:

> *"The earliest manuscripts and some other ancient witnesses do not have verses 9–20."*

Mark 16:14–20 is fiction, and although James will be proven to have witnessed Jesus resurrected at least three times from other accounts, we do not have his written words proving him a witness.

7. THE DISCIPLES WITH THOMAS (JOHN 20:26–29)

> 24 But Thomas, one of the twelve, called Didymus, wasn't with them
> when Jesus came. 25 The other disciples, therefore, said to him, "We
> have seen the Lord!" But he said to them, "Unless I see in his hands
> the print of the nails, put my finger into the print of the nails, and
> put my hand into his side, I will not believe." 26 After eight days,
> again his disciples were inside and Thomas was with them. Jesus
> came, the doors being locked, and stood in the middle, and said,
> "Peace be to you." 27 Then he said to Thomas, "Reach here your
> finger, and see my hands. Reach here your hand, and put it into
> my side. Don't be unbelieving, but believing." 28 Thomas answered
> him, "My Lord and my God!" 29 Jesus said to him, "Because you
> have seen me, you have believed. Blessed are those who have not
> seen and have believed." 30 Therefore, Jesus did many other signs in
> the presence of his disciples, which are not written in this book; 31
> but these are written that you may believe that Jesus is the Christ,
> the Son of God, and that believing you may have life in his name.

Analysis: Thomas wasn't in the locked room with the disciples when Jesus first appeared to them. He heard their testimony but didn't believe them. Like the rest of the disciples, Thomas would not believe that Jesus had resurrected until he observed it himself. Eight days after Jesus' resurrection and his appearance to the disciples without Thomas, Jesus again appeared to his disciples—this time with Thomas present. The doors were again locked when Jesus stood in the middle of them and stated the same words, "Peace be to you." This is exactly how Jesus previously appeared eight days ago in the locked room.

In his previous appearance, Jesus had the disciples visibly inspect his execution wounds to prove to them that it was him. Jesus did the same here; he had Thomas touch his wounds to prove to him that Jesus had risen from the dead. This is evidence that Jesus, like in the previous appearances, kept himself from being recognized. Therefore, this account has been validated through Jesus and John, who documented it.

8. SEVEN DISCIPLES AT THE SEA OF TIBERIAS (JOHN 21:1–23)

> 1 After these things, Jesus revealed himself again to the disciples
> at the sea of Tiberias. He revealed himself this way. 2 Simon Peter,
> Thomas called Didymus, Nathanael of Cana in Galilee, and the
> sons of Zebedee, and two others of his disciples were together. 3

> Simon Peter said to them, "I'm going fishing." They told him, "We are also coming with you." They immediately went out and entered into the boat. That night, they caught nothing. [4] But when day had already come, Jesus stood on the beach; yet the disciples didn't know that it was Jesus. [5] Jesus therefore said to them, "Children, have you anything to eat?" They answered him, "No." [6] He said to them, "Cast the net on the right side of the boat, and you will find some." They cast it therefore, and now they weren't able to draw it in for the multitude of fish. [7] That disciple therefore whom Jesus loved said to Peter, "It's the Lord!" So when Simon Peter heard that it was the Lord, he wrapped his coat around himself (for he was naked), and threw himself into the sea. [8] But the other disciples came in the little boat (for they were not far from the land, but about two hundred cubits away), dragging the net full of fish. [9] So when they got out on the land, they saw a fire of coals there, with fish and bread laid on it. [10] Jesus said to them, "Bring some of the fish which you have just caught." [11] Simon Peter went up, and drew the net to land, full of one hundred fifty-three great fish. Even though there were so many, the net wasn't torn. (John 21:1–11)

Analysis: I only presented the first portion of the event because within it is the evidence proving this appearance by Jesus to be valid. The eighth recorded resurrection event is the third recorded appearance to the disciples, and it is full of eyewitness details. For example:

- *John stated seven disciples were present, and he named five of them and even provided extra details about Thomas and Nathanael.*
- *Peter "wrapped his coat around him [Jesus](for he was naked),"*
- *"The other disciples came in the little boat (for they were not far from the land, but about two hundred cubits away),"*
- *"They caught nothing," even though they fished all night,*
- *"Jesus stood on the beach; yet the disciples didn't know that it was Jesus." and,*
- *They counted the fish, totaling 153.*

It is very strange for John to tell you the names of five of the seven disciples who witnessed Jesus' resurrection. John providing extra details about Thomas and Nathanael, then leaving off the names of two disciples for a resurrection account, is very weird for John, who understood and emphasized the importance of eyewitness testimony. It's so strange, in fact, that it didn't happen—John provided their names, and false teachers edited them out. The two unnamed disciples of Jesus were men whom the false teachers didn't want you to know, just like they didn't want you to know the name of the other man on the road whom Jesus appeared to. Again, the only candidate that comes to mind is the secret disciple of Jesus named Nicodemus. If Nicodemus were to be documented here and Jesus appearing to him on the road, this religious leader would be very special, and the Gospel of Matthew would obviously be his testimony.

There are numerous specific eyewitness details presented in this event, AND Jesus is initially disguised from being recognized. In addition, with the identity of the two unnamed disciples known, John has placed the other two eyewitnesses who documented their own testimony, James and Nicodemus, as observing this event too. This is a valid resurrection appearance.

DOCUMENTED RESURRECTION TESTIMONY

1. Jesus is God born as a man with a mission to start the NC (6 BC)
2. Satan attempted to stop the NC from starting (6 BC)
3. Jesus' mission to teach, heal and perform miracles (26–30 AD)
4. Jesus' sacrifice and resurrection (30 AD)
    a. Luke 24:33–49, John 20:19–23—Jesus testified to this account because he was hidden from view and then revealed himself later. There are numerous situational eyewitness details presented by Nicodemus, and John's testimony supports this appearance to be valid resurrection testimony
    b. John 20:26–29—Jesus testified to this account because he was hidden from view, then revealed himself later, and John provided eyewitness situational details, so it is a valid testimony of Jesus' resurrection
    c. John 21:1–23—Jesus testified to this account because he was hidden from view, then revealed himself later, and John provided numerous eyewitness situational details, so it is a valid Jesus' resurrection testimony
5. Second half of Jesus' seven-year mission (30–33 AD)
6. Start of the NC, the Great Tribulation, and the AOD (33 AD)

7. Generation of the Disciples (33–67 AD)
8. The NC (33–2333 AD)
9. First half of the NC—the reign of the Beast (33–1333 AD)
    a. Mark 16:14–20—There is no description of what Jesus looked like, how the disciples responded, nor where this event took place. There are no situational eyewitness details presented, and Jesus isn't in disguise to later reveal himself, so it is fiction
10. Second half of Jesus' NC—Jesus' 1000-year reign with his chosen ones (1333–2333 AD)
11. The Time of the End (2333-?)
12. Judgement

21

A Resurrection Miracle—Part 3

THE NEXT TWO RESURRECTION accounts to be reviewed are those written by Saul, also called Paul:

9. Saul's Claim for Peter, James, and the Apostles (1 Corinthians 15:3–8)
10. Saul, also called Paul (Acts 9:3–20, 22:6–16, and 26:12–18)

The three accounts listed together for Saul in Acts are different versions of the same story; therefore, they will be analyzed together and compared.

9. SAUL'S CLAIM FOR PETER, JAMES, AND THE APOSTLES (1 CORINTHIANS 15:3–8)

> 3 For I delivered to you first of all that which I also received: that
> Christ died for our sins according to the Scriptures, 4 that he was
> buried, that he was raised on the third day according to the Scrip-
> tures, 5 and that he appeared to Cephas, then to the twelve. 6 Then
> he appeared to over five hundred brothers at once, most of whom
> remain until now, but some have also fallen asleep. 7 Then he ap-
> peared to James, then to all the apostles, 8 and last of all, as to the
> child born at the wrong time, he appeared to me also.

Analysis: Saul's words, "and last of all, as to the child born at the wrong time, he appeared to me also," make it crystal clear that Saul claimed Jesus visited him after Jesus was executed and came back from the dead. There are three summary accounts of this referenced appearance presented in Acts, and I will analyze them next. Here I want to address Jesus' appearances to the others that Saul has claimed.

First, Saul wrote that Jesus appeared to "Cephas [Peter] THEN to the twelve." There aren't twelve, and there is no documentation that Jesus appeared to Peter before the disciples. There is that claim in Luke 24:33–35 that the two men on the road showed up to tell the disciples about Jesus appearing to them, and they found everyone talking about how Jesus appeared first to Peter. But there is nothing to support that claim besides this comment by Saul, and Paul is making a claim that he couldn't have witnessed because he was "a child born at the wrong time." The eyewitnesses documented that Jesus first appeared to Mary Magdalene, then to Nicodemus and Cleopas on the road, so I don't have any reason to doubt them to believe Saul. Saul has not told the truth.

There is already enough here to claim this summary by Saul to be fiction, but before I complete this analysis, I want to address the statement Saul made that "then he appeared to James, then to all the apostles." Through this comment, Saul has indicated that James was an apostle, then Jesus appeared to the rest of the apostles, then to Saul as an apostle born at the wrong time. The term "apostle" is very important here because with it, Peter, one of Jesus' chosen disciples, has been grouped with the rest of the "apostles."

Jesus did not endorse his brother James because he commanded his disciple John to take care of his mother. Saul's words are not the word of God, but as an apostle, he and James will be like Peter. It isn't a coincidence that the two men Saul named that Jesus appeared to, along with himself, were the only two men he claimed met with him when, after three years of teaching Jesus, he decided to seek out the disciples (Galatians 1:18–19).

Saul has grouped himself in with the apostles—a group of men including James, the brother of Jesus, whom he claimed Jesus appeared to. This fraud investigator is smelling something fishy with the term "apostles" because Jesus' brother James and Paul are using this term to be put on a level playing field with the disciples Jesus chose. A search of the word "apostles" revealed that it is used twice in the three eyewitness testimony Gospels. First, Matthew 10:2 describes the twelve "apostles," but this summary was copied from Mark, then edited by false teachers with the designation "apostles" added in, so it is a false teacher edit. The only other mention of "apostles" in the three eyewitness testimonies is strange:

> *29 When his disciples heard this, they came and took up his corpse and laid it in a tomb. 30 The APOSTLES gathered themselves together to Jesus, and they told him all things, whatever they had done, and whatever they had taught. 31 He said to them, "Come away into*

a deserted place, and rest awhile." For there were many coming and going, and they had no leisure so much as to eat. (Mark 6:29–31)

The disciples have obtained JB's body and entombed it, then the verse Mark 6:30 comes out of nowhere without connecting to the surrounding verses. It's obviously a false teacher edit; therefore, both mentions of "apostles" in the Gospels outside of Luke are false teacher edits.

The term apostle was slipped into the Gospels with those two edits in Matthew and Mark, then the false teachers warmed you up with six references in Luke, the second-hand book with the stolen Nicodemus resurrection account. Then, now that the false teachers exposed you to that term "apostle," they mentioned it another 71 times in the letters and edited it into Revelation three times. The false teachers have programmed followers of Jesus to believe that "apostles" have been moved by the Holy Spirit, so they can speak for God. Having James, Jesus' brother, as one lends the term and concept credibility. Saul, as an apostle, has gained authority to speak for God—but that authority didn't come from God; it came from false teachers. You will see later how the Holy Spirit ensured that you understand the term "apostles" was used to facilitate the false teacher coup of the NC.

10. SAUL, ALSO CALLED PAUL (ACTS 9:3–20, 22:6–16, AND 26:12–18)

As usual, I've separated the three accounts into actions to compare the details to each other to determine the truthfulness of Saul's claims:

1. Saul Sees a Light

Acts 9:3
As he traveled, he got close to Damascus, and suddenly a light from the sky shone around him.

Acts 22:6
"As I made my journey, and came close to Damascus, about noon, suddenly a great light shone around me from the sky."

Acts 26:12–13
[12] "Whereupon as I traveled to Damascus with the authority and commission from the chief priests, [13] at noon, O king, I saw on the

> way a light from the sky, brighter than the sun, shining around me and those who traveled with me."

Analysis: The author of Acts stated in the first account, "as HE traveled," as "HE got close to Damascus," and a light "shone around HIM." The next two accounts are presented in the first person, as though Saul is describing what he saw and the author is writing it down, or the author witnessed Saul making these claims. We can be assured that the author is with Saul for the last two accounts because the author stated he was:

> *When THEY had come opposite Mysia, THEY tried to go into Bithynia, but the Spirit didn't allow THEM. (Acts 16:7)*

> *When he had seen the vision, immediately WE sought to go out to Macedonia, concluding that the Lord had called US to preach the Good News to them. (Acts 16:10)*

Prior to Acts 16:10, the author of Acts was not with Saul. The first account is written before Acts 16:10, so the author is not an eyewitness; he doesn't state who described the event, and the author of Acts is unidentified. It is at best second-hand information; therefore, I will omit Acts 9:3–20 from this analysis to focus on Saul's words in the other two accounts.

Saul added the detail in his meeting with the king that he had official "authority and commission from the chief priests." Paul's trip to Damascus was sanctioned by the religious leaders whom Jesus frequently rebuked and denounced. To this fraud investigator who found that Saul's words were inserted into the Bible even though they weren't the word of God, and that Saul provided a resurrection account that has been proven to be a lie (1 Corinthians 15:3–8), Saul's trip, being sanctioned by false teachers, is troubling. In his first account, Saul observed "a great light shone around me from the sky." For the king, Saul changed his story to say the light was "shining around me and those who traveled with me." Saul's story has changed.

2. Reactions and Jesus' Words

> Acts 22:7
> "I fell to the ground, and heard a voice saying to me, 'Saul, Saul, why are you persecuting me?'"

Acts 26:14
"When we had all fallen to the earth, I heard a voice saying to me in the Hebrew language, 'Saul, Saul, why are you persecuting me? It is hard for you to kick against the goads.'"

Analysis: Saul claimed in his first account that "I fell to the ground," but in the second account, he stated that "we had all fallen to the earth." He has again extended the effects of the experience on everyone who was there, rather than just himself. In addition, when Saul repeated his story for the king, he embellished the words of Jesus by adding "It is hard for you to kick against the goads," and stated that Jesus spoke to him in the "Hebrew" language." I have concerns with Saul's story because he provides no eyewitness details. A person hearing the voice of God will remember exactly what God said to him, how the voice sounded, and describe his emotions when he heard the voice. Was the voice loud? Did it thunder? Was it commanding? Did it come out of the sky like described in Mark 1:11 and 9:7? After Saul heard this voice, did he talk to the others to ask them about what they saw and heard? Saul provided three very general situational details; he saw a bright light, fell, then heard a voice, and all three of those general descriptions have changed over time. Saul has told two very brief stories that present no eyewitness situational details, such as 'it happened by the tree', or 'big rock', or something, anything, and his two stories don't match.

3. Saul's Response

Acts 22:8
"I answered, 'Who are you, Lord?'"

Acts 26:15
"I said, 'Who are you, Lord?'"

Analysis: Why would a Pharisee who is persecuting followers of Jesus and on a mission on behalf of those who hated Jesus, ask God who he is? Saul says he heard a voice but did not describe that voice, then he responds to that voice by asking God a question with only one possible response. Saul is either going to hear, 'It's God' or 'It's Jesus,' and I'll bet you know in advance which answer it was. It's beginning to seem like Saul was on a sanctioned, planned trip of deception.

4. Jesus' Response to Saul

Acts 22:8–10
"He said to me, 'I am Jesus of Nazareth, whom you persecute.' [9]
"Those who were with me indeed saw the light and were afraid,
but they didn't understand the voice of him who spoke to me. [10] I
said, 'What shall I do, Lord?' The Lord said to me, 'Arise, and go
into Damascus. There you will be told about all things which are
appointed for you to do.'"

Acts 26:15–19
"He said, 'I am Jesus, whom you are persecuting. [16] But arise, and
stand on your feet, for I have appeared to you for this purpose: to
appoint you a servant and a witness both of the things which you
have seen, and of the things which I will reveal to you; [17] delivering
you from the people, and from the Gentiles, to whom I send you,
[18] to open their eyes, that they may turn from darkness to light
and from the power of Satan to God, that they may receive remission of sins and an inheritance among those who are sanctified by
faith in me.' [19] "Therefore, King Agrippa, I was not disobedient to
the heavenly vision, [20] but declared first to them of Damascus, at
Jerusalem, and throughout all the country of Judea, and also to the
Gentiles, that they should repent and turn to God, doing works
worthy of repentance.

Analysis: There is deception detected in the first version because Saul is a man who claimed to hear the word of God, and the first thing he remembered and mentioned was what happened to those around him. There is zero chance of a real appearance by God being described in this manner. A person knocked down to the ground by a bright light, then hearing the voice of God, would be in awe and full of emotions. Saul didn't describe his emotions because he would have had to make them up. He projected his made-up experience on those around him because he had no reaction or memory of what happened. Whenever Jesus appeared resurrected, he testified to it himself by being hidden at first, then later he revealed himself. Jesus was not hidden from Saul; therefore, Jesus did not testify that he appeared to Saul.

Saul tells the story twice, and they are nothing alike, proving earlier conclusions that he made up his Jesus' appearance story. In the first account, Jesus tells Saul to "go to Damascus" to receive further instructions on what Jesus wanted Saul to do. Saul completely forgot his earlier account because later Saul tells the King that the voice of Jesus gave him explicit details of everything Jesus wanted him to do. According to the account he gave the king, there wasn't a reason for Saul to continue his journey to Damascus to get further instructions from Jesus on what he was to do because Jesus gave him the instructions he was supposed to get in Damascus. Saul's account is a lie, and we know why, because he explained it to the King. Saul was commissioned by the religious leaders to infiltrate the NC to assist them in taking control of it. This story provided the foundation for Saul to claim to be a Christian.

Note that the only information we have about Saul is from Saul and his companion, who went on a missionary journey with him and recorded the details in Acts. Everything we read about Saul is presented through the words of Saul in his own letters and the words of a companion. There is no independent information from Jesus' chosen eyewitnesses that describes Saul. Some may claim that Peter mentioned Saul in his letter named 2 Peter, but the wording in that letter indicates Saul is likely the author or, at a minimum, a contributor to it.

I bring this up because Saul is revered in every Christian church I've attended. Was Saul always a false teacher, or did he try to spread the word of God sincerely to recruit others to follow Jesus? I'll try to answer that from an analysis of the following information provided by Saul.

Immediately after Saul claimed Jesus appeared to him, he started his churches. Through Saul's letters, we read how he presented himself as a lover of Jesus, willing to do anything to prove himself to be a loyal follower. Yet Saul made little effort to meet with those Jesus chose to be his eyewitnesses:

> [18] Then after three years I went up to Jerusalem to visit Peter, and stayed with him fifteen days. [19] But of the other apostles I saw no one except James, the Lord's brother. [20] Now about the things which I write to you, behold, before God, I'm not lying. (Galatians 1:18–20)

Consider that for three years Saul says he taught about Jesus, but he had never met Jesus, nor heard the words of Jesus, nor did he interact with those who did. Saul stated that after three years, he finally went to Jerusalem to meet with Jesus' chosen disciples and eyewitnesses. But what happened during that meeting? We don't know because Saul provided zero situational details of this fifteen-day period he supposedly spent with Peter. What did Peter and Saul talk about? Where were they staying? We know that Peter and Andrew lived in a house together (Mark 1:29), but Saul did not provide any description of the living accommodation, nor did he mention any verbal exchange or meeting he had with Peter. Saul wrote that he met with Peter, an eyewitness to Jesus, but that was the end of it because he provided no details.

Saul claimed that he also met with "James, the Lord's brother." Do you find it odd that Saul claimed that only two met with him on this visit, and they just happened to be the two men Saul mentioned by name who Jesus appeared to, along with the apostles and Saul? I do. To top it off, at the end of that summary, Saul stated, "I'm not lying." Why would Saul worry about people thinking he is lying? Because that is what Saul does, he lies. His resurrection story was a lie, and he lied about the appearances of Peter and James. He also lied about Jesus appearing to "apostles," as you will soon see. Saul has a history of not telling the truth. Imagine spending fifteen days with Peter, who witnessed Jesus, then having nothing to say about those fifteen days. Sounds ridiculous when you consider it that way, doesn't it?

Then we learn from Saul's letters that he was rejected by the disciples for the next fourteen years:

> Then after a period of fourteen years I went up again to Jerusalem with Barnabas, taking Titus also with 4me. (Galatians 2:1)

Consider that Saul has been teaching Jesus for seventeen years, but never spent time with Jesus' chosen eyewitness, except for one vague encounter he claimed he had with Peter, but provided no details for. The documentation indicates that there was no effort by Saul to join the mission of Jesus' chosen disciples.

Saul was doing his own thing without the disciples, and he was content with his solo mission:

> But from those who were reputed to be important—whatever they were, it makes no difference to me; God doesn't show partiality to man—they, I say, who were respected imparted nothing to me, (Galatians 2:6)

Saul stated that Jesus' chosen disciples were "reputed to be important," and "imparted nothing to me." Saul thought the leadership of Jesus' chosen disciples was questionable, and the ones Jesus chose and taught had nothing to offer him. Just in case you didn't pick up on Saul questioning the authority of Jesus' chosen disciples, he mentioned it again:

> and when they perceived the grace that was given to me, James and Cephas and John, those who were reputed to be pillars, gave to Barnabas and me the right hand of fellowship, that we should go to the Gentiles, and they to the circumcision. (Galatians 2:9)

Again, Saul referred to Jesus' chosen eyewitnesses as "reputed to be pillars" of the NC movement. According to Saul, some others may have thought John, Peter, and Andrew had something to offer followers of Jesus, but Saul didn't agree. The truth about Paul is that he was an arrogant loner who claimed to love Jesus but despised the disciples Jesus chose.

Saul is the guy who most Christians hold in high esteem, yet I don't understand why. Saul's words are not the word of God; he lied about Jesus appearing to him, disputed the leadership of Jesus' chosen disciples, and commented that they couldn't teach him anything. To top it off, Saul was arrogant enough to build his reputation at the cost of Peter:

> When Cephas came to Antioch, I opposed him to his face, because he stood condemned. (Galatians 2:11)

Saul questioned the disciples' leadership, then publicly rebuked Peter in front of a crowd (Galatians 2:14). Wow! Saul publicly disrespected Jesus' chosen eyewitnesses, and the reason he explained for it might make sense to some, but consider that only one side of the story is presented. We don't really know what happened or what was said because Saul lies and builds his own reputation. Saul wasn't welcomed by the disciples because they didn't believe his story of Jesus appearing to him, and they considered him to be a false teacher. Based on the evidence, I agree with the disciples.

The Holy Spirit went out of the way to warn you about Saul, too. We all know when and how Jesus changed Simon's name to Peter—it was public and documented well. But Saul's name change came with much different circumstances:

> But Saul, who is also called Paul, filled with the Holy Spirit, fastened his eyes on him, (Acts 13:9)

There are very interesting details embedded in the story about Saul's name change that you need to be aware of. Saul's name change to Paul is slipped into the middle of a story about a false teacher named Bar Jesus, who was also called "Elymas the sorcerer" (Acts 13:6–12). That false teacher with two names "was an attendant of the proconsul, "Sergius Paulus." In the story, Sergius Paulus witnessed Saul confront Elymus, the false teacher. Saul told the false teacher with two names that, because of his false teaching, he would go blind. It came true as Sergius Paulus watched, so Paulus believed in Jesus. Hmmm, "Sergius PAULUS" sounds a lot like Paul, and according to the first account of Saul's conversion in Acts 9:3–20, Saul was blinded by Jesus. Elymus, the false teacher with two names, was blinded in Acts

13:6–12, and Paulus believed, then Saul with two names (Acts 13:9) was blinded in Acts 9:3–20, and he believed. The stories of Saul and Elymus are nearly exactly alike.

Saul was sent by the religious leaders to infiltrate the NC and take control of it. John told us that Saul and his co-conspirators were successful because the disciples were led astray just as Jesus had warned them in the Olivet Discourse. The only reason Saul is the center of attention in the Christian Bible is that false teachers needed a legitimate avenue to speak for God, and God didn't give them one, so they created it through Saul, and as you will see, the term "apostles." Much of the Church's logistics comes from Paul. ART theology comes to us based on the words of Saul. Most importantly, sharing your possessions and supporting the church are addressed through Saul, too.

Without Saul, the church has only Jesus, and that isn't enough for most CRLs in a corrupted NC church. Walk into a church and claim that you want the words of Jesus, but you don't want the words of Saul, or rather Paul, and I can guarantee from my experiences that you will be shown the door.

DOCUMENTED RESURRECTION TESTIMONY

1. Jesus is God born as a man with a mission to start the NC (6 BC)
2. Satan attempted to stop the NC from starting (6 BC)
3. Jesus' mission to teach, heal and perform miracles (26–30 AD)
4. Jesus' sacrifice and resurrection (30 AD)
5. Second half of Jesus' seven-year mission (30–33 AD)
6. Start of the NC, the Great Tribulation, and the AOD (33 AD)
7. Generation of the Disciples (33–67 AD)
8. The NC (33–2333 AD)
9. First half of the NC—the reign of the Beast (33–1333 AD)
    a. 1 Corinthians 15:3–8—Saul's claims of Jesus appearing to Peter, James and "apostles" is fiction because there are no situational eyewitness details presented, Jesus is not disguised then revealed later, so he hasn't testified to the truth of any of them, and there is a clear motive for these to promote Saul as an "apostle,"

   b. Acts 22:6–16, 26:12–18—This resurrection account is fiction because there are no situational eyewitness details presented, Jesus does not first appear in disguise, then reveal himself, so he has not testified for this account, and the vague descriptions provided by Saul in the two accounts contradict each other

10. Second half of Jesus' NC—Jesus' 1000-year reign with his chosen ones (1333–2333 AD)

11. The Time of the End (2333-?)

12. Judgement

22

A Resurrection Miracle—Part 4

THERE ARE ONLY TWO additional resurrection accounts yet to be analyzed, and they are:

11. Jesus appears to others for over forty days (Acts 1:3)
12. Jesus appears to "them" (Acts 1:4–9)

At first glance, it may appear as though I've separated one resurrection appearance, Acts 1:3–9, into two separate events. They are addressed separately because Acts 1:3 is a stand-alone resurrection summary statement that has a very powerful connection to Daniel prophecy, while Acts 1:4–9, together with Acts 1:2, will be proven to be a false teacher creation:

11. JESUS APPEARS TO OTHERS OVER FORTY DAYS (ACTS 1:3)

> To these he also showed himself alive after he suffered, by many proofs, appearing to them over a period of forty days, and speaking about God's Kingdom. (Acts 1:3)

Acts 1:3 states that it applies "To these," but the described group of people can only be identified through the previous two verses:

> [1] The first book I wrote, Theophilus, concerned all that Jesus began both to do and to teach, [2] until the day in which he was received up, after he had given commandment through the Holy Spirit to the apostles whom he had chosen. (Acts 1:1–2)

Analysis: Acts 1:2 states that "these" men described in Acts 1:3 who witnessed Jesus resurrected over forty days, are "apostles whom he had chosen." Through the statement "To these he also showed himself alive" in Acts 1:3, the author has connected the "Holy Spirit" and chosen "apostles" to the eyewitness disciples that Jesus chose. Per these three verses, apostles became just like disciples. Until you get to this resurrection appearance account in Acts, as reported earlier, there is no documentation of Jesus in the three eyewitness testimonies choosing apostles to add to his disciples.

Throughout the Gospel testimonies, we have no doubt that Jesus chose "disciples" to be his eyewitnesses who would also observe his resurrection. John noted that Jesus appeared to the disciples with Thomas eight days after his first resurrection appearance to the disciples. Also, John told us that Jesus gave the disciples many other signs that he was alive (John 20:30–31). Immediately after that comment, John provided many eyewitness details about Jesus' appearance to seven of his disciples at the Sea of Tiberias. Based on John's documentation, a forty-day period of resurrection appearances to Jesus' disciples is not only possible but also likely to be true.

Since Acts 1:3 is a general resurrection statement, the normal criteria for determining it to be valid don't apply. Jesus will not be providing his testimony through first appearing in disguise, then revealing himself later, nor will I find eyewitness details in it to prove it to be true. Furthermore, it's presented in an account by an author who admitted he was not an eyewitness. But God had unconventional evidence in mind when the Holy Spirit had one of Jesus' eyewitnesses document Acts 1:3.

The forty days of Jesus' resurrection appearances are proven through their connection to Daniel 12:11–12. Recall the earlier analysis that proved Daniel 12:11 to describe how God decreed 1290 days for Jesus' eyewitnesses to document their testimony. At that time, I put off the analysis of Daniel 12:12 until later because, in addition to being connected to the 1290 days of testimony documentation, it is also connected to the forty days of resurrection appearances (Acts 1:3):

> [12] *Blessed is he who waits, and comes to the one thousand three hundred thirty-five days. (Daniel 12:12)*

Daniel 12:12 that follows Daniel 12:11 presents a number that is remarkably close to the 1290 days of Daniel 12:11. The blessing of some men described as being 1335 days is 45 days more than the decreed 1290 days for the disciples to document their testimony.

Jesus' Holy Spirit was with the disciples as they wrote their testimony, so they were certainly blessed during the 1290 days. The 40 days of appearances through Acts 1:3 would have happened just prior to Jesus' disciples documenting their testimony, and they certainly were blessed to witness Jesus during that time, too. Those two periods account for a total of 1330 days (1290+40), and this is 5 days short of 1335. The sacrifice of Jesus came before the 40 days of appearances, and the disciples would have been blessed to witness this, too. But earlier, we calculated 6.75 days for the time of the sacrifice:

- *Portion of a day—Sunday—At suppertime, Jesus is anointed as the sacrifice 6 days before Passover Day (John 12:1–3)*
- *Full day—Monday—Jesus preparing for his sacrifice*
- *Full day—Tuesday—Jesus preparing for his sacrifice*
- *Full day—Wednesday—Jesus preparing for his sacrifice*
- *Full day—Thursday—Arrest and Trial*
- *Full day—Friday—Jesus executed as the sacrifice on Preparation Day and placed in the tomb late that day (John 19:42)*
- *Full day—Saturday—Sabbath and Passover Day; Jesus is in the tomb*
- *Portion of a day—Sunday—Resurrection Day, Jesus first appeared to Mary sometime after the tomb was found empty that morning (John 20:14)*

If you closely examine the sacrifice of Jesus, you will notice that Jesus was in the tomb for 1.75 days over a three-day period (John 2:19).

When Jesus was in the tomb, the disciples didn't witness him. Therefore, subtract the 1.75 days that the disciples didn't witness Jesus when he was in the tomb from the days of his sacrifice, and the disciples witnessed Jesus for 5 days during his sacrifice. Together, we have the following days of Jesus' chosen disciples witnessing Him:

5 days of Jesus' sacrifice+40 days of appearances+1290 days with Holy Spirit = 1335 days

Of all the people who have ever existed, only Jesus' chosen disciples were blessed to witness Jesus' sacrifice, 40 days of resurrection appearances, and have the Holy Spirit with them over a 1290-day period to document their testimony of Jesus. Only Jesus' disciples fulfilled Daniel 12:11–12 and Acts 1:3.

To provide their testimony of Jesus, the disciples needed to be with and observe Jesus. Therefore, not only did they witness the sacrifice and the last half of Jesus' seven-year mission, but they would also have had to witness Jesus' teaching, preaching, and performing works. In summary, Daniel 12:12 describes the disciples of Jesus who witnessed him fulfill his entire seven-year Messiah mission, as described through Daniel 9:24–27 prophecy. The testimony of John and Daniel, together with the Holy Spirit, has provided literal and mathematical testimony proving Acts 1:3 to be the truth. Acts 1:3 is a proven resurrection summary validating Jesus' forty days of appearances to his disciples, and this also proves John's statement in John 20:30–31 to be true.

But Daniel 12:12 and the forty days of appearances through Acts 1:3 do not apply to "apostles" unless all apostles are the disciples. This apparent contradiction with Acts 1:2 is addressed through analysis of the last resurrection appearance described in Acts 1:4–9.

12. JESUS APPEARS TO THEM (ACTS 1:4–9)

> [4] Being assembled together with them, he commanded them, "Don't depart from Jerusalem, but wait for the promise of the Father, which you heard from me. [5] For John indeed baptized in water, but you will be baptized in the Holy Spirit not many days from now." [6] Therefore, when they had come together, they asked him, "Lord, are you now restoring the kingdom to Israel?" [7] He said to them, "It isn't for you to know times or seasons which the Father has set within his own authority. [8] But you will receive power when the Holy Spirit has come upon you. You will be witnesses to me in Jerusalem, in all Judea and Samaria, and to the uttermost parts of the earth." [9] When he had said these things, as they were looking, he was taken up, and a cloud received him out of their sight. (Acts 1:4–9)

Analysis: Jesus promised the Holy Spirit to his disciples to help them document their eyewitness Jesus' testimony (John 14:26), then he fulfilled that promise on the first evening of his resurrection day (John 20:22). Acts 1:8 tells us that Jesus has promised a group of apostles that "you will receive power when the Holy Spirit has come upon you." Through THIS resurrection appearance documentation, Jesus has promised to send the Holy Spirit to the APOSTLES WHO ARE NOT disciples. Furthermore, Acts 1:8 states that Jesus will send the apostles the Holy Spirit so that they "will be witnesses to me. . .to the uttermost parts of the earth." This command is the same one that Jesus gave to his four chosen eyewitness disciples (Mark 13:9–11). This resurrection account is presented to make the "apostles" be just like Jesus' "disciples."

Jesus gave his eyewitness disciples authority to testify on his behalf, and that makes their words the word of God. Acts 1:2 and 1:4–9 have extended this authority to apostles who aren't disciples. With apostles made to be like disciples, they also can speak and write the word of God through Jesus. But apostles never witnessed Jesus alive, nor did they witness him crucified and dead, so they cannot testify to him being resurrected. In addition, apostles never witnessed Jesus teach, nor did they witness Jesus perform miracles. Jesus didn't appoint apostles because they did not meet Deuteronomy 18:18–22, 17:6, and 19:15 requirements to have God's authority to speak for him.

The contradiction with apostles being called disciples found through analysis of Acts 1:3 proves that the "apostle" authority, like disciples, is fictional. An examination of Acts 1:2 and 4–9 to search for witness validation of it proves the account to be a false teacher creation:

- *There aren't any situational eyewitness details presented.*
- *Jesus has not testified on his behalf by first being hidden, then revealing himself later, and,*
- *The author admitted that he is not an eyewitness to Jesus, and he doesn't provide the source of this resurrection appearance description.*

There is zero eyewitness testimony proving this resurrection appearance to be truthful.

As reported earlier, if you remove both the fictional "apostles" reference in James' testimony (Mark 6:30) and the edit of the listing of the twelve in Nicodemus' testimony (Matthew 10:2) that was copied from James (Mark 3:13), the only Gospel mentioning "apostles" is Luke. Then the term "apostle" is mentioned more frequently than "disciple" in Acts. The emphasis on apostles in Acts and in Saul's letters reinforces the false teacher's attempt to normalize apostles to be just like disciples.

Acts 1:8 stated that Jesus gave the apostles the authority to speak for God, just like he did for his disciples. False teachers created "apostles" and packaged the words of the "apostles" side by side with the words of Jesus, then placed them into the Bible. Through that action, Deuteronomy 18:18–22. 17:56, and 19:5 requirements from God for who God allowed to speak for him, were expanded to men inspired by the Holy Spirit. The false teachers who claimed to own the NC through Peter claimed they could speak for God. They still make this claim as described in their Catholic Catechism #80 and #81.

Through Acts 1:3, the Holy Spirit told you not to trust the word "apostles" like you trust the disciples. Combine Acts 1:1–2, 4–9 resurrection fiction with the false claims of Saul's resurrection appearance and the massive amount of evidence predicting an NC coup, and you will be convinced that God knew the future in advance. Through prophecy, God told you all the details of the NC in advance. Like my "Billford" vision, prophecy is evidence presented in advance, and it has all been proven true.

DOCUMENTED RESURRECTION TESTIMONY

1. Jesus is God born as a man with a mission to start the NC (6 BC)
2. Satan attempted to stop the NC from starting (6 BC)
3. Jesus' mission to teach, heal and perform miracles (26–30 AD)
4. Jesus' sacrifice and resurrection (30 AD)
    a. Acts 1:3, John 20:30–31—The testimony of John, together with the Holy Spirit and Daniel, who provided literal and mathematical evidence, validate Jesus appearing to his disciples over a 40-day period
5. Second half of Jesus' seven-year mission (30–33 AD)
6. Start of the NC, the Great Tribulation, and the AOD (33 AD)
7. Generation of the Disciples (33–67 AD)
8. The NC (33–2333 AD)
9. First half of the NC—the reign of the Beast (33–1333 AD)
    a. Acts 1:4–9—False teachers created this fictional account because there are no situational eyewitness details presented, Jesus is not in disguise then revealed later to testify, and the account states that the Holy Spirit is designating "apostles" as eyewitnesses, but they haven't witnessed Jesus
10. Second half of Jesus' NC—Jesus' 1000-year reign with his chosen ones (1333–2333 AD)
11. The Time of the End (2333-?)
12. Judgement

23

The Complete Jesus Evidence Package

THE WORLD HAS THE following testimonies of Jesus' resurrection that are proven to have been observed by at least two or three witnesses:

- Jesus first appeared to Mary Magdalene at the tomb of Jesus on the first day of Jesus' resurrection.
- Next, on the first day of his resurrection, Jesus appeared to Nicodemus and Cleopas on the road, then spent time with them at a house to teach them all about the Good News.
- Later that evening on the first day of Jesus' resurrection, Jesus appeared to his disciples, but without Thomas.
- Eight days later, at the same locked location, Jesus appeared to Thomas and the disciples.
- Sometime later, Jesus appeared to seven of Jesus disciples at the Sea of Tiberias.

Only two or three eyewitness testimonies of Jesus' resurrection are required. We have Mary Magdalene as an eyewitness documented by James and John, and Nicodemus and John, who provided their own testimony. Jesus is also an eyewitness to his resurrection in each of those accounts because he first appeared in disguise, then later revealed himself. James documented that he observed the eyewitness testimony of Mary Magdalene and the two men on the road, and we know that he was present to witness Jesus' resurrection on three occasions. But false teachers removed and replaced James' personal resurrection testimony, so we do not have records of his statements.

In summary, less James' testimony that has been replaced with a fictional account, and counting Jesus as an eyewitness, we have four confirmed eyewitnesses through five documented resurrection appearances. In addition, there is one statement claiming that Jesus appeared to his disciples over a forty-day period, and that has also been proven to be true. The evidence to prove that Jesus resurrected himself overwhelmingly exceeds the burden of proof specified by God in Deuteronomy 17:6 and 19:15.

On the flip side, we have proven false teacher resurrection editing. Resurrection accounts in the Gospels of Matthew and Mark, and the ones by Paul in 1 Corinthians and Acts, were analyzed and found to be fiction. Furthermore, false teachers removed the valid resurrection account written by Nicodemus from his eyewitness testimonial, the Gospel of Matthew, and placed it into the Gospel of Luke to give that Gospel credibility. They also removed the valid resurrection account presented in Acts 1:3 from one of the eyewitness testimonies and inserted it into Acts, then combined it with a fictional "apostle" resurrection account. We can be certain too that false teachers removed James' testimony of Jesus resurrected and replaced it with the fictional accounts provided at the end of Mark 16.

The summary below presents the evidence proving that Jesus is the resurrected Son of God who was the one-time sacrifice for sin. The evidence below also proves the widespread NC corruption by false teachers for personal gain. False teachers who Jesus referred to as "beasts" spread and grew very powerful to control the NC and much of society. Jesus warned that the beast would morph into, "BABYLON THE GREAT, THE MOTHER OF THE PROSTITUTES AND OF THE ABOMINATIONS OF THE EARTH" (Revelation 17:5). The beasts who were the founders of the Catholic Church, are referred to as the "MOTHER OF THE PROSTITUTES" because their peddling of their words they claimed came from God, allowed sin and profiteering to spread throughout numerous future Christian church denominations. As the "MOTHER" of prostitutes and the source of the AOD, their offshoots became what Jesus referred to as "BABYLON THE GREAT." Babylon is representative of the Protestant portion of the NC church, with thousands of denominations that embrace their own brand of religion through their own doctrine. Each organization is separate from the others, and they aren't one flock as Jesus commanded, yet each claims to have the true knowledge of Jesus as they battle for membership.

The complete evidence package proving Jesus and that statement from Revelation is summarized in the following:

JESUS COMPLETE EVIDENCE PACKAGE

1. Jesus is God born as a man with a mission to start the NC (6 BC)
    a. Deuteronomy 18:20–22—Prophets who prophesied the coming of Jesus spoke for God
    b. Matthew 5:17—The OT prophets prophesied Jesus and spoke for God (e.g., Isaiah 7:14, Micah 5:2, Zachariah 12:10, Hosea 11:1, Plasm 22:18, and Malachi 3:1, et al)
    c. Matthew 26:56—Jesus came to fulfill OT prophets' prophecy
    d. John 5:46—Moses prophesied about Jesus and spoke for God
    e. Revelation 6:1–2—The first seal, Jesus comes to the world
    f. Daniel 2:32, 44—Jesus born, lived, and completed his mission during in the Silver Kingdom (562 BC-33 AD), with some rulers Godly and others following evil
    g. Daniel 4:10–12—Jesus is the tree of life that came to the world so that "all flesh was fed from it"
    h. Daniel 7:4, 14—Jesus has everlasting dominion with a permanent Kingdom
    i. Daniel 9:25—There were "sixty-two sevens," 434 years from the last Messiah prophecy Malachi 3:1–3 to Jesus' birth, who as the "seven sevens" always existed
    j. Revelation 21:2—Jesus is the "New Jerusalem," the replacement of the OC with the NC with a Kingdom that will last forever.
    k. Revelation 12:1–2—God sent a Messiah to the world to start the NC that is referred to in Revelation as a "woman"
2. Satan attempted to stop the NC from starting (6 BC)
    a. Revelation 6:3–4—The second seal, Satan comes to the world to stop Jesus
    b. Matthew 2:1–20—Satan pursued Jesus as a child, but God protected Jesus
    c. Daniel 7:5—The second beast is Satan who came to the world to destroy the NC and keep people from being redeemed through the blood of Jesus

d. Daniel 8:8—Out of the OC came a powerful group of Jewish leaders who formed their own religion with rules and regulations that didn't come from God

e. Revelation 12:3–5—Very early in Jesus' life, Satan, with a great following, attempted to stop Jesus' seven-year mission from happening to start the NC, but Satan failed

f. Matthew 1:18—2:20—Satan failed to eliminate and stop Jesus

3. Jesus' mission to teach, heal and perform miracles (26–30 AD)

   a. John 5:31, 34, 8:13, 17–18—Jesus affirmed that he must be proven through eyewitness testimony in accordance with Deuteronomy 17:6 and 19:15

   b. John 10:24–25—God has testified on behalf of Jesus through his works

   c. John 3:34, 8:58, 10:30, 12:49–50, 14:24—Jesus claimed to speak for God and stated he was God

   d. John 14:25–26—Jesus promised his eyewitnesses that he would provide them with help to remember everything Jesus said and did, and to explain all the details

   e. Mark 13:5–6—Jesus warned his disciples that they would be led astray and train false teachers who would then lead many people astray with their teaching

   f. Mark 13:3, 10—Jesus selected four disciples, James, John, Peter, and Andrew, to be his eyewitnesses to document their testimony for all people of the world

   g. Mark 5:36–43, 9:2–4, 13:1–37, 14:32–42—Jesus took his eyewitnesses with him privately to observe all the details of his life, to ensure their testimony is complete

   h. Daniel 9:27—The first half of Jesus' seven-year mission to have his chosen eyewitnesses observe him teach and perform works to prove he was the Messiah

   i. Revelation 12:6—God protected Jesus and his eyewitness disciples for 1260 days—Jesus' mission days are equal to the 1260 days the two witnesses testified for Jesus

j. Revelation 12:7–10—Satan, working with false teachers, continues their attacks on Jesus, but through the blood of Jesus, his disciples overcame evil to testify

k. John 1:7, 15, 19, 32, 34, 5:31–38, 8:13–18, and 10:24–25—The author emphasized the importance of eyewitness testimony

l. John 11:1—12:17 and 20:5–7 provide a few of the numerous situational eyewitness details proving that he was with Jesus and observed his teaching and miracles

m. John 13:23–25—John was close to Jesus and was in the seat of honor as he leaned against "against Jesus' chest" and asked Jesus a question on behalf of Peter

n. John 21:2—Only two disciples of Jesus are left unnamed, the Zebedee brothers, and the author must be one of them

o. John 1:37, 13:23, and 19:25–27—The unnamed Zebedee was very special to Jesus

p. John 12:27–29, Mark 3:17—Jesus named John and James Zebedee the Sons of Thunder to reveal them both as writing the testimony that validates Jesus as God

q. Mark 13:3—With Andrew and Peter being unable to write and chosen as the two witnesses of Revelation 11, and John having documented the Gospel of John, James must be the author of the Gospel of Mark

r. Mark 1:19–20—The author of Mark provided Zebedee household eyewitness details that would come from one of the Zebedee brothers

s. Mark 1:29–31—One of numerous events copied by Matthew's author, indicating that the author of Mark is a trusted eyewitness of Jesus

t. Mark 1:19–20, 29–31, 5:37, 9:2—James, who was present with the other inner circle disciples is proven to have authored the Gospel of Mark

u. Mark 1:30, 3:16—The author referred to Peter as Simon in Mark 1:30 because he hadn't heard Jesus' change Simon's name to Peter until Mark 3:16

v. Mark 10:35–41—The Zebedee brothers were the only ones present; therefore, the eyewitness testimony had to come from James

w. John 3:1–21, 7:50–51, 19:39–42—Nicodemus was being taught and connected to Jesus

x. Matthew 5:1—7:29—Nicodemus sat in the audience to hear Jesus' sermon that addressed subjects of interest to a religious leader

y. John 7:53—8:11—Removed and replaced to hide Nicodemus from being recognized by his response to a Pharisee challenge to investigate Jesus as the Messiah

z. Matthew 27:1–66—Numerous eyewitness details of religious leader interaction with Judas the traitor, Jesus' interrogators, the tomb guards proving him to be one

aa. Mark 6:45–52 and John 6:16–26—James and John witnessed the miracle of Jesus' walking on water and calming a storm

ab. Mark 6:35–45, and John 6:4–15—James and John, two eyewitnesses who were present, observed Jesus' miracle to feed 5000 with five loaves of bread and two fish

ac. Matthew 14:15–21—Nicodemus again copied an account from James (feeding 5000) indicating that he believed what James wrote was factual

ad. John 6:7–9—The disciples are split up, and Andrew was again with John, who was with Jesus, proving that Andrew was close to Jesus and was an inner circle disciple

4. Jesus' sacrifice and resurrection (30 AD)

   a. John 20:21–22—Jesus delivered the promised Holy Spirit on resurrection day to help his eyewitnesses get their testimony exact

   b. Daniel 9:27—As the replacement for the Holy City, Jesus' permanent sin sacrifice in the middle of his seven-year mission, made people forever righteous

   c. Revelation 12:11—Jesus' disciples triumphed over Satan and the false teachers by witnessing Jesus' sacrifice, so that they will testify even to death

   d. John 12:1–3, 19:31,42, 20:1, 14—Together, these passages prove Jesus' sacrifice is exactly 6.75 days

e. Mark 9:31—Jesus' promise to rise on the third day has been fulfilled

f. John 19:25–27—Jesus assigned his mother to John, indicating that Jesus' brothers, including James, were not disciples of Jesus nor would they follow him later

g. Matthew 27:48–50, Mark 15:36–37, John 19:28–30—Two eyewitnesses, James and John, recorded Jesus dying on the cross; he said his last words and gave up his spirit and Nicodemus coped it from James indicating that he believed Jesus died

h. Matthew 27:51–53, Mark 15:38–41, John 19:31–35—There is evidence of tampering with James' and Nicodemus' accounts of what happened after Jesus' death

i. John 19:38–39—Nicodemus is documented with Joseph entombing Jesus' body; therefore, he witnessed Jesus as having died on the cross

j. Mark 16:9–11, John 20:14–18—Jesus testified to this account because he was hidden from view and then revealed himself later. John, who placed himself with Mary, documented her testimony that presents eyewitness situational details, and James validated that he heard Mary's testimony, so it is a valid testimony of Jesus' resurrection testimony

k. Mark 16:12–13, Luke 24:13–32—Jesus testified to this account because he was hidden from view and then revealed himself later. Nicodemus, as one of the two men, provided numerous eyewitness situational details, and James validated that he heard his testimony, so it is a valid Jesus' resurrection testimony

l. Luke 24:33–49, John 20:19–23—Jesus testified to this account because he was hidden from view and then revealed himself later. There are numerous situational eyewitness details presented by Nicodemus, and John's testimony supports this appearance to be valid resurrection testimony

m. John 20:26–29—Jesus testified to this account because he was hidden from view, then revealed himself later, and John provided eyewitness situational details, so it is a valid Jesus' resurrection testimony

n. John 21:1–23—Jesus testified to this account because he was hidden from view, then revealed himself later, and John provided numerous eyewitness situational details, so it is a valid Jesus' resurrection testimony

o. Acts 1:3, John 20:30–31—The testimony of John, together with the Holy Spirit and Daniel, who provided literal and mathematical evidence, validates Jesus' appearing to his disciples over a 40-day period

5. Second half of Jesus' seven-year mission (30–33 AD):

   a. Mark 13:10—assignment given to James, John, Peter, and Andrew to provide their testimony

   b. Mark 13:31—The words of Jesus will remain unchanged throughout all time

   c. Daniel 9:27—The second half of Jesus' seven-year mission, to give his chosen eyewitnesses the Holy Spirit of God to help them complete their testimony

   d. Daniel 12:7—The testimony of Jesus' eyewitnesses will save many and it will happen during a "time, times and half a time"

   e. Daniel 12:10–11—The "time, times, and half a time" correspond to the 1,290 days between when the daily sacrifice is abolished and the abomination that causes desolation

   f. Revelation 1:1–2, 1:4, 1:9, 22:8—John Zebedee, who received Revelation from Jesus, was special, stated his name, and confirmed his previous testimony

   g. Revelation 12:12–13—Satan knew he only had a short time to attack Jesus' chosen disciples to prevent their testimony from being documented to start the NC

   h. Revelation 12:14—God protected the eyewitness disciples from harm for a "time, times, and half a time," which is about 3-1/2 years and correlates to 1290 days

   i. Daniel 12:7—The words a "time, times, and a half" correlate to Revelation 12:14

   j. Daniel 12:10–11—With God's protection between Jesus' sacrifice and the AOD, there are exactly 1290 days decreed for the disciples to document their testimony

k. John 12:1–3, 19:31, 42, and 20:1, 14—Jesus' sacrifice is exactly 6.75 days long

l. Daniel 9:27—Through Revelation 12:14, Daniel 12:7, 10–11, and words of John, the decreed seven-year mission of Jesus to start the NC is proven exactly 2556.75 days

m. John 19:35–37 and John 21:24—John, the disciple of Jesus, testified that he had provided his testimony of Jesus, and he wrote the Gospel of John with his own hand.

n. James wrote his testimony in a book now referred to as the Gospel of Mark

o. Nicodemus, an old man who was a secret disciple of Jesus, documented his testimony in a book that is now referred to as the Gospel of Matthew

6. Start of the NC, Great Tribulation, and the Testimonies are completed (33 AD)

   a. Mark 13:9, 11—persecution of the disciples starts

   b. Mark 13:14—Jesus' chosen eyewitnesses will observe the AOD as the false teachers replace the temple of Jesus with their brand of religion

   c. Daniel 4:16–17—With seven indicating something complete, Jesus' Kingdom will last forever, "let seven times pass over him"

   d. Daniel 9:26–27—The false teachers with Satan will commit the AOD that will replace Jesus' permanent sacrifice with themselves claiming to speak for God

   e. Daniel 11:31–32 –False teachers with Satan replace Jesus NC with themselves, referred to as the AOD

   f. Revelation 12:15–16—Immediately after God's protection of the disciples ceased, false teachers claimed to be God, and followers of evil agreed

   g. Revelation 12:17—Satan and the false teachers made war with the followers of Jesus

7. Generation of the Disciples (33–67 AD)

   a. Mark 13:9, 11—Jesus foretold the persecution and executions of his four inner circle disciples John, Andrew, Peter, and James

b. Mark 13:28–31—The generation of the disciples will start the NC with their testimony that will spread to all nations, but they will also witness false teachers take control of it and destroy it

c. Acts 12:2—James is executed for Jesus

d. 1 John 2:18–19—Those the disciples chose to succeed them were false teachers, antichrist, who were taking over the NC

e. Revelation 11:1–12—The mission of the two witnesses is to welcome the Gentiles into the NC

f. Revelation 11:2—False teachers and Satan trample on the Holy City for 42 months

g. Revelation 11:3–5—Peter and Andrew burn Rome and are transferred to Jerusalem, where they prophecy for 1,260 days—the same number of days as Jesus' mission

h. Revelation 11:7–8—Andrew and Peter, as the two witnesses, are executed

i. Revelation 13:1–10—Jesus refers to the false teachers together with Satan as the beast who persecutes and executes anyone who doesn't accept their reign

j. Revelation 13:11–17—Another beast comes out of the first beast to speak on their behalf

k. Revelation 13:3, 14—The beasts took their authority from Peter, one of the two witnesses they executed

l. Revelation 13:5—42 months of persecution connect the beast to Peter, one of the two witnesses of Revelation 11:1–3, as the beast's path to possess the woman

m. Revelation 1:1–2, 1:4, 1:9, 22:8—John received and documented a vision about the future

n. 1 Corinthians 15:3–8—Saul's claims of Jesus appearing to Peter, James and "apostles" is fiction because there are no situational eyewitness details presented, Jesus is not disguised then revealed later so he hasn't testified to the truth of any of them, and there is a clear motive for these to promote Saul as an "apostle"

o. Acts 22:6–16, 26:12–18—This resurrection account is fiction because there are no situational eyewitness details presented, Jesus does not first appear in disguise then reveal himself so he has not testified for this account, and the vague descriptions provided by Saul in the two accounts contradict each other

8. The NC (33—2333 AD)
    a. Deuteronomy 17:6, 19:15—Once Jesus' mission is completed, two- or three-witnesses are required per the Law of God to prove him to all future nations and people
    b. Matthew 24:1–35—False teachers edited the copied version of the Olivet Discourse in Matthew to support ART theology and hide the beast in the time of the end
    c. Mark 13:31—Jesus promised to forever protect his words from corruption
    d. John 2:4, 4:21—Jesus referred to the NC as being an hour long, but this is per the eternal time clock
    e. 1 John 2:18—John confirmed that the NC is an hour long per eternity time
    f. Daniel 2:34–35—Jesus is the rock that came in the Silver/Bronze Kingdom interface to replace all other rulers over the people of God during the NC; it will last forever
    g. Daniel 7:6–8—The third beast, the bronze rulers, were given dominion given from God to reign over the people of God, and they appointed a fourth beast, and their corruption will last throughout the NC
    h. Daniel 8:8–14—The religious leaders who trampled on Jesus and his disciples took away Jesus' sacrifice through their AOD, and corrupted the 2300 years of the NC
    i. Daniel 9:26–27—The false teachers and Satan will destroy the NC to the end of time when those responsible will have the wrath of God poured out on them
    j. Revelation 17:3–6—The false teachers who Jesus called the "beasts" and "The Mother of the Prostitutes and of the Abominations of the Earth," corrupted the NC
    k. John 7:30, 8:20—The NC is an hour long per the eternal clock

9. First half of the NC—the reign of the Beast (33—1333 AD)
    a. Acts 8:1—The great tribulation started with the stoning death of Stephen
    b. Mark 13:5-6—False teachers will lead the disciples astray, take control of the NC, then, by claiming they are Jesus, will lead many people astray
    c. Mark 13:15-20—Jesus foretold the great tribulation also called the great persecution
    d. Mark 13:21-25—False teachers who Jesus referred to as the beast will remove the light of the world and persecute anyone who doesn't submit to their reign
    e. Revelation 6:5-6—The third seal describes the bread of life and the living water of Jesus provided by those in charge of the NC being in short supply
    f. Revelation 6:7-8—The fourth seal, the false teachers persecute and execute those who reject their message from Satan, with a bit of Jesus' words mixed in
    g. Revelation 6:9-10—The fifth seal tells of the ruthless leaders starting to execute those who reject their message
    h. Revelation 6:12-17—The sixth seal reveals that false teachers working with Satan have completely removed Jesus, the light of the world, from the NC
    i. Revelation 7:1-17—The decreed number of martyrs, 144000, has been executed as the false teacher's reign of terror, referred to as the great tribulation, ends
    j. Daniel 2:32, 39—The Bronze Kingdom false teachers who took control of the NC by claiming to speak for Jesus rule over the people of God
    k. Daniel 4:13-14—Ruthless false teachers claiming to be God during the Bronze Kingdom cut down the tree because they wanted the NC for themselves
    l. Daniel 7:11—The two beasts rule over the people of God with an iron fist as they claim to be able to speak for God

m. Daniel 11:33–39—False teachers use Jesus' sanctuary for profit, control of property, and wealth; some followers of Jesus will fight back and lose their lives

n. Revelation 13:1–17—The beasts persecuted and executed everyone who objected to their NC authority and reign, and forced everyone to worship them

o. Revelation 14:1–5—The beast executed 144,000 blameless followers of Jesus who were virgins because they rejected the sinful woman

p. ECFs eliminated James as the author of an eyewitness testimony referred to now as the Gospel of Mark, and stated that John Mark wrote down Peter's words in it

q. ECFs eliminated Nicodemus as the author of an eyewitness testimony and renamed it after a disciple named Matthew, whom they created to observe events they edited

r. Matthew 16:12–21—False teachers edited Nicodemus' copy of James' observation of this event to create Jesus assigning Peter to reign over the NC on their behalf

s. Matthew 14:22–32—False teachers edited the account of Jesus walking on water by adding Matthew 14:28–31 that describes Peter also walking on water

t. Mark 5:36–43, 9:2–4, 14:32–42—ECFs edited Andrew out of being one of Jesus' inner circle disciples to elevate Peter's standing among the disciples

u. Matthew 9:9–11—ECFs edited a copied version of the tax collector story to claim Matthew as the author of the Gospel of Nicodemus

v. Matthew 10:2–4 and Mark 3:14–19—ECFs inserted a list of the twelve disciples in Mark, copied it into Matthew, and noted that Matthew was the tax collector

w. ECFs edited many copied verses in the Gospel of Matthew to have it appear as though their created author, Matthew, observed the events

x. ECFs made numerous edits to NT documentation to emphasize Peter and separate him from the rest of the disciples (e.g., Mark 16:7, Luke 24:33–34, etc.)

y. ECFs inserted Saul's letters into the Bible to give the beast leaders authority to speak for God, just like they claimed Saul had. ECFs and RCLs created theology to hide the deceit of the false teachers (e.g., ART, Daniel 9:27 to be the great tribulation, John dying in prison at an old age, etc.)

z. Matthew 28:7–10—This resurrection account has no situational eyewitness details, a muted reaction by those witnessing it, and it contradicts other resurrection accounts; therefore, it is a false teacher-created account

aa. Matthew 28:16–20—Clearly, a false teacher created an account to validate Matthew 28:7–10 because there is no description of Jesus, the eyewitnesses had nothing to say, the content contradicts John 2:22, and there are no situational eyewitness details

ab. Mark 16:14–20—There is no description of what Jesus looked like, how the disciples responded, nor where this event took place. There are no situational eyewitness details presented, and Jesus isn't in disguise to later reveal himself, so it is fiction

ac. Acts 1:4–9—False teachers created this fictional account because there are no situational eyewitness details presented, Jesus is not in disguise then revealed later to testify, and the account states that the Holy Spirit is designating "apostles" as eyewitnesses, but they haven't witnessed Jesus

10. Second half of Jesus' NC—Jesus' 1000-year reign with his chosen ones (1333–2333 AD)

    a. Mark 13:26–27—Jesus returns in the clouds with his chosen ones

    b. Mark 13:26–27—Jesus foretold the end of the great tribulation with a spiritual return in the clouds to free the Gospel from the grips of the beast

    c. Revelation 8:1—The seventh seal denotes the second half hour of the NC, starting as heaven goes silent because Jesus makes his spiritual return to the NC

    d. Revelation 20:4–5—There is a transition in the NC with the return of Jesus, who will reign with the 144000 martyrs for 1000 years.

    e. Revelation 8:3–6—The prayers of people during the 1000-year reign of Jesus are rejected, indicating a time of trouble, and seven trumpet blasts will explain why

f. Revelation 8:7—The first trumpet is a message of fire and brimstone that has CRLs focused on punishment rather than eternal life through Jesus

g. Revelation 8:8–9—God meets with his people on a mountain, but the second trumpet describes something like a mountain—CRLs are pretending to be Jesus

h. Revelation 8:10–11—Like wood-destroying pests and bitter water, the living water and word of God through Jesus, described in the third trumpet, is infested with theology and words of men

i. Revelation 8:12—The fourth trumpet is about carefully crafted, cherry-picked messages of CRLs who ignore Jesus to mislead people through their message

j. Daniel 2:33, 40–43—A mixed Kingdom of Iron and Clay with a fractured mess of numerous Christian faith denominations, who will reign side by side throughout

k. Daniel 4:15—Jesus as the stump and roots of the tree remained "even with a band of iron and bronze," signifying the Iron/Clay Kingdom with the return of Jesus

l. Daniel 7:12–13—God took away the beasts' authority, and Jesus returned to rule over God's mixed people, with some following God and others following evil

m. Daniel 11:40–45—The battle between the people of God and Satan for the NC will last until the end of time

n. Revelation 14:6 –Jesus returned to free the Good News from the beasts and removed their authority to rule over the NC; they no longer rule, but they aren't eliminated

o. Revelation 14:7–20—Jesus warns people to make the right choice and reject the beast to be blessed, or follow the beast to face the wrath of God and be punished

11. The Time of the End (2333-?)

a. Revelation 1:7—The tribes of the earth who have rejected Jesus will witness him coming in the clouds, and because of their punishment, they will mourn

b. Revelation 8:13—The last three trumpets will highlight three woes that will befall those who have rejected Jesus

c. Revelation 20:1–3—Satan is set free for a short while after his 1000 years in the pit of the Abyss during Jesus' reign is over

d. Revelation 9:1–11—The wrath of God is poured out on those following Satan; the agony of this fifth trumpet is so bad that they will seek death, but God won't allow it

e. Revelation 9:12—The five months of the fifth trumpet are the passing of the first woe

f. Revelation 9:13–21—Plagues, war, and the fire of God are poured out during this undefined time when the wrath of God is poured out on the inhabitants of the earth

g. Revelation 20:7–9—Satan, with his 200 million-strong army, controls the world and attacks the few remaining followers of Jesus who are in a camp

h. Daniel 12:1—The time of the end will be a miserable existence

i. Revelation 13:18—The "666" connects those following the beast to John 6:66 as those who reject Jesus and are judged and condemned

j. Revelation 15:1—16:1—At the time of the end, the last part of the second half of the NC, God will pour seven bowls of wrath out on those who follow the beasts

k. Revelation 16:2–16—God pours out six bowls of wrath on the beast, then Jesus warns that he will return like the thief in the night to end Satan's war on Jesus

l. Revelation 16:17–21—The end is described with no followers of Jesus left on the earth, and large hailstones representing bombs destroy the world

12. Judgement

a. John 3:18—Believe in Jesus and you are not judged, reject and you have been judged

b. Revelation 10:1—11:13—The second woe is for those who have rejected the testimony of Jesus and the two witnesses, because they are immediately condemned

c. Revelation 11:14—The third woe is the judgment and condemnation of those who have rejected Jesus that comes quickly after the second woe

d. Daniel 7:9–10—Jesus has an eternal kingdom, and the NC will end in judgment for those who corrupted it

e. Daniel 12:1–4—Those with their name in the book of life will be rewarded, and those left out will feel everlasting contempt

In summary, it's an overwhelming evidence package that proves Jesus as God who came as the sin sacrifice for all the people of the world so that whoever believes in him will have eternal life!

24

The Eternal Kingdom

As described earlier, Jesus came to remove the eternal death sentence we all have through sin. Some will have that death sentence removed to spend eternity with God in peace, as my friend who died from cancer and appeared to me in the spirit had. Jesus stated that the gate that "leads to life" is narrow (Matthew 7:13–14) and only a few will enter it, so all your efforts while you are living in your body should be focused on making sure you enter through that narrow gate. Others will reject Jesus' redemption offer only to be judged guilty, repeated here for emphasis:

> He who believes in him is not judged. He who doesn't believe has been judged already, because he has not believed in the name of the only born Son of God. (John 3:18)

Deniers of Jesus are judged as soon as they reject Jesus, so their names are not found in the book of life.

I was on the fence about believing in Jesus because I needed evidence, and during my NDE, I witnessed a dreadful glimpse of an eternal existence. Jesus told me through my NDE that I was condemned because I was a lukewarm Christian:

> So, because you are lukewarm, and neither hot nor cold, I will vomit you out of my mouth. (Revelation 3:16)

I had periodically attended a Christian church, and I read my Bible daily, searching for answers. In fact, I had even professed my faith in Jesus nearly thirty years before my NDE, but it didn't matter because I never fully embraced following Jesus. I should have known what I was facing because Jesus warned me, but I wasn't listening.

Had God not spared me from death as a lukewarm believer in Jesus, I would have been condemned to an eternity of pain and suffering. Attending a church or being a nice person who reads the Bible won't get you through the narrow gate, nor will dedication to a particular religious organization:

> 9 Another angel, a third, followed them, saying with a great voice, "If anyone worships the beast and his image, and receives a mark on his forehead or on his hand, 10 he also will drink of the wine of the wrath of God, which is prepared unmixed in the cup of his anger. He will be tormented with fire and sulfur in the presence of the holy angels and in the presence of the Lamb. (Revelation 14:9–10)

With the Catholic Church and the pope as their leader, together referred to as the beast, on the surface, it appears as though Jesus is telling the world that Catholics will have the wrath of God poured out on them.

This concept troubled me because some of my family members are dedicated to the Catholic Church. Furthermore, my father, who was a praying man with a heart of gold, had died about 40 years earlier as a Catholic. The possibility of my father being eternally condemned when he apparently tried so hard to follow Jesus through the Catholic Church was troubling. I prayed for clarity and received the following dream in response:

> August 30, 2022—We were out for a ride on the golf cart and came back to the condo where the work was going on in the kitchen and entrance. Julio has been contracted to do the work and in the dream my dad is working side-by-side with Julio in our condo.

I knew that Julio was alive because he was working in my condo. Therefore, there is only one possible message coming from the Holy Spirit in this dream: my father was also alive! The Holy Spirit had shown me through that dream that my father entered through the narrow gate, even though he was a member of the Catholic Church. His name was written in the book of life.

I had received a clear message through the word of God and that dream that a person's affiliation with any specific Christian organization did not guarantee or eliminate that person's entry through the narrow gate. This concept also applies to Christians following Jesus through offshoots of the Catholic Church—the "Prostitutes" from Revelation 17:5, and to the rest of the NC church:

> Another, a second angel, followed, saying, "Babylon the great has fallen, which has made all the nations to drink of the wine of the wrath of her sexual immorality." (Revelation 14:8)

Babylon is representative of the 40,000-plus denominations of Christianity that all have their own doctrine and theology and also claim to be the Christians who truly understand the word of God. Jesus called them no better than the "Mother of Prostitutes" and all who follow their CRLs, doctrine, and theology rather than Jesus will feel the wrath of God. Worshipping and dedicating your life to anything but Jesus puts your salvation in jeopardy.

I've already stated from the word of God several times that those who accept Jesus are not judged and enter through the narrow gate, and those who reject Jesus have already been judged and will eternally die. But then there is the following description of judgment that seems to contradict those words of Jesus:

> I saw the dead, the great and the small, standing before the throne, and they opened books. Another book was opened, which is the book of life. The dead were judged out of the things which were written in the books, according to their works. [13] The sea gave up the dead who were in it. Death and Hades gave up the dead who were in them. They were judged, each one according to his works. [14] Death and Hades were thrown into the lake of fire. This is the second death, the lake of fire. [15] If anyone was not found written in the book of life, he was cast into the lake of fire. (Revelation 20:12–15)

Since followers of Jesus are not judged and those who rejected Jesus have already been judged, this judgment must be for others.

There are two categories of people who are judged "according to their works." The sea is the living water of Jesus—the word of God, so the "great" (Revelation 20:12) must be those who died following the word of God. The small must be for those who died and are in "Death and Hades" waiting to be "cast into the lake of fire." Since they are being judged, the "great" must have followed the word of God without knowing who Jesus was. Likewise, the small never rejected Jesus, but they took a different path—they followed evil. The great and small are those who never heard the words of Jesus throughout their lifetime, and they will be judged on their works from the history kept in the set of books that is not the book of life. Neither you nor I can specify the criteria or judgment details of this group—it is up to God.

One thing we do know is that some will be judged for their actions—but that won't be you if you are a believer in Jesus. If you truly believe in Jesus, God knows that your actions will reflect your faith.

God has shown that he is just and will only allow those into heaven who want to be with him and praise him for eternity. Those who praised God throughout their lifetime will fit right in in heaven; therefore, we should be joyous to have the possibility of other Jesus lovers with us for eternity. Those who follow evil never praised God during their lifetimes, and they don't belong in heaven. The "second death" awaits them.

Now is the time to ensure your faith in Jesus is solid. If you believe nothing else from the evidence package and are convinced that theology and church doctrine are the way to Jesus, make sure you include belief in Jesus' seven-year mission:

DANIEL 9:24–27, THE SEVENTY SEVENS OF JESUS

1. 6 BC: There were "sixty-two sevens" and "seven sevens" between the last OT prophecy for the Messiah and the birth of Jesus. Sixty-two sevens is the 434 years from Malachi 3:1–3, which was received in 440 BC, and Jesus existed during that period, even before his birth, so he is the "seven sevens." Jesus' mission as the Messiah and God was to repeal the permanent sentence of death for the people of all nations (Deuteronomy 17:6, 18:17–22, 19:15).
2. 26–30 AD: The first half of the 'seven-year' mission of Jesus consisted of him preaching, teaching, healing, and performing miraculous works for 1260 days. During this time, God protected Jesus and his disciples (Revelation 12:6) from false teachers and Satan (Revelation 12:3–12). The following specific references to eyewitness testimony prove that God protected Jesus and his disciples during this 1260 day-long period because Jesus had a set time for his sacrifice (Matthew 12:14, 16:21, 17:22–23, 20:18–19, 21:46; Mark 3:6, 9:31, 10:33–34; John 2:4, 7:6, 7:30, 10:39, 12:23, 17:11). The two witnesses, Peter and Andrew, had a symbolic testimony for 1260 days.
3. 30 AD: In the middle of the 'seven', the Anointed One, Jesus, was put to death (Daniel 9:27 and the citations for Jesus' sacrifice listed above for Jesus' first half of his mission). Jesus also promised to return from the dead to appear to his disciples (e.g., Matthew 23:39; Mark 9:1; John 14:18–19, 16:16 et al).

4. 6.75 days: There were 6.75 days decreed for Jesus' sacrifice. Jesus' sacrifice consisted of his anointing, the last supper, Jesus' trial and execution, the time Jesus spent in the grave, then the instant he rose from the dead and appeared to others proving that he had resurrected himself (calculated from John 12:1–3, 19:42, 20:1–20).
5. 40 days: Jesus' eyewitness disciples were blessed to observe Jesus for 1335 days (Daniel 12:12) during his sacrifice (5 days without the 1.75 days Jesus spent in the tomb), resurrection (40 days), and document their testimony (1290 days).
    1. Jesus appeared to Mary Magdalene (Mark [James] 16:9–11, John 20:11–17)
    2. Jesus appeared to Nicodemus and Cleopas (Mark [James] 16:12–13, Luke 24:13–32 [that section written by Nicodemus])
    3. Jesus appeared to the disciples (John 20:19–25 and Luke 24:36–53 [that section written by Nicodemus])
    4. Then Jesus appeared to the disciples with Thomas (John 20:26–29)
    5. Seven disciples witnessed Jesus at the Sea of Tiberias (John 21:1–23)
    6. The disciples had many more undocumented Jesus resurrected appearances John 20:30–31 and 21:25)
    7. The blessed group of disciples observed Jesus resurrected for forty days (Acts 1:3)
6. 30–33 AD: The "time, times, and half a time" (Revelation 12:14) corresponds to the 1290 days (Daniel 9:26–27, 12:11–12) God protected (Mark 13:9–13, Revelation 12:11–14) his group of chosen disciples (Mark 13:3 and Luke 14:25–27) who had the Holy Spirit (John 14:26, 20:22) with them to help them document their testimony (Mark 13:10)
7. 33 AD: The testimonies of Jesus were completed in 33 AD by eyewitnesses whom Jesus selected (Mark 13:3, 10; Luke 14:25–27; John 7:50–52):
    - The Gospel of Matthew, written by Nicodemus
    - The Gospel of Mark was written by James
    - The Gospel written by John

> Their testimony documentation of Jesus completed the transition from the OC to the NC (Revelation 12:14). The Kingdom of God on earth through Jesus was finalized on the last day of that decreed seven-year period (Daniel 2:44, 8:4, 9:24–27), which, as calculated earlier, took exactly 2556.75 days.

Jesus has assured you that if you believe he is God and came to the world as the one-time sacrifice to remove the stain of sin, you will have eternal life. The evidence package found and presented throughout this investigation PROVES that Jesus is who he claimed to be. Daniel described the promise of God to provide redemption for all his people, and he fulfilled that promise through Jesus.

For you, religious leaders and followers of Jesus who are wondering about the NC church and what it is supposed to be, I think Jesus provided us with the details of this in Revelation. Through that vision, John witnessed one throne of God rather than two because Jesus is God (Revelation 4:1–3). The twenty-four elders represented the crystal-clear word of God from the Law given to the twelve tribes of Israel and through the testimony of the twelve disciples of Jesus (Revelation 4:4–5). John saw four creatures at the throne representing the Holy Spirit, who sees everything and is the interface between the throne of God and the NC church (Revelation 4:6–8). The NC church is to have one function only, and that is to praise Jesus as God (Revelation 4:9–11) to help people get their names in the book of life (Revelation 5:1–14). Then, as presented earlier, Jesus provided John with the details of how redemption of the people of all nations will be found through the testimony of the two witnesses (Revelation 10:1—11:19), and all the future details of a corrupted NC in an overwhelmingly evil world (Revelation 6:1—9:21 and 12:1—16:21).

If you have been on the fence about dedicating your life to Jesus, I hope these results have convinced you to get off the fence and choose wisely to believe. If you were already a believer, your faith has been reinforced because the Gospels are eyewitness testimonies presented by those who were with Jesus, and you can believe their testimony. I investigated all the details of the story of Jesus, and I believe and I hope you do too. The choice is yours, and I hope you follow the evidence to Jesus.

Be Wise and God Bless,
Jaz

www.ingramcontent.com/pod-product-compliance
Lightning Source LLC
LaVergne TN
LVHW050634100826
845148LV00011B/1863

* 9 7 9 8 3 8 5 2 7 0 4 4 6 *